Praise for

"Must have information for business executives." - Alex Wilmerding, Principal, Boston Capital Ventures

"Great information for both novices and experts." - Patrick Ennis, Partner, ARCH Venture Partners

"Want to know what the real leaders are thinking about now? It's in here." - Carl Ledbetter, SVP & CTO, Novell, Inc.

"Priceless wisdom from experts at applying technology in support of business objectives." - Frank Campagnoni, CTO, GE Global Exchange Services

"A wealth of real world experience from the acknowledged industry leaders you can use in your own business." - Doug Cavit, CTO, McAfee.com

"An incredible resource of information to help you develop outside-the-box..." - Rich Jernstedt, CEO, Golin/Harris International

"What C-Level executives read to keep their edge and make pivotal business decisions. Timeless classics for indispensable knowledge." - Richard Costello, Manager-Corporate Marketing Communication, General Electric (NYSE: GE)

"The Inside the Minds series is a valuable probe into the thought, perspectives, and techniques of accomplished professionals. By taking a 50,000 foot view, the authors place their endeavors in a context rarely gleaned from text books or treatiese." - Chuck Birenbaum, Partner, Thelen Reid & Priest

"True insight from the doers in the industry, as opposed to the critics on the sideline." - Steve Hanson, CEO, On Semiconductor (NASDAQ: ONNN)

"Unlike any other business books, Inside the Minds captures the essence, the deep-down thinking processes, of people who make things happen." - Martin Cooper, CEO, Arraycomm

"The only useful way to get so many good minds speaking on a complex topic." - Scott Bradner, Senior Technical Consultant, Harvard University

www.Aspatore.com

Aspatore Books is the largest and most exclusive publisher of C-Level executives (CEO, CFO, CTO, CMO, Partner) from the world's most respected companies. Aspatore annually publishes a select group of C-Level executives from the Global 1,000, top 250 professional services firms, law firms (Partners & Chairs), and other leading companies of all sizes. C-Level Business Intelligence™, as conceptualized and developed by Aspatore Books, provides professionals of all levels with proven business intelligence from industry insiders – direct and unfiltered insight from those who know it best – as opposed to third-party accounts offered by unknown authors and analysts. Aspatore Books is committed to publishing a highly innovative line of business books, and redefining such resources as indispensable tools for all professionals. In addition to individual best-selling business titles, Aspatore Books publishes the following lines of unique books, reports and journals: Inside the Minds, Executive Reports, and C-Level Quarterly Journals. Aspatore Books is a privately held company headquartered in Boston, Massachusetts, with employees around the world.

Inside the Minds

The critically acclaimed *Inside the Minds* series provides readers of all levels with proven business intelligence from C-Level executives (CEO, CFO, CTO, CMO, Partner) from the world's most respected companies. Each chapter is comparable to a white paper or essay and is a future-oriented look at where an industry/profession/topic is heading and the most important issues for future success. Each author has been carefully chosen through an exhaustive selection process by the *Inside the Minds* editorial board to write a chapter for this book. *Inside the Minds* was conceived in order to give readers actual insights into the leading minds of business executives worldwide. Because so few books or other publications are actually written by executives in industry, *Inside the Minds* presents an unprecedented look at various industries and professions never before available.

INSIDE THE MINDS

INSIDE THE MINDS:
The Ways of the VC

*Leading Venture Capitalists on Identifying Opportunities,
Assessing Business Models & Establishing Valuations*

Published by Aspatore, Inc.
For corrections, company/title updates, comments or any other inquiries please email info@aspatore.com.

First Printing, 2003
10 9 8 7 6 5 4 3 2 1

ISBN 1-58762-217-3

Inside the Minds Managing Editor, Carolyn Murphy, Edited by Michaela Falls, Proofread by Eddie Fournier, Cover design by Scott Rattray & Ian Mazie

If you are a C-Level executive interested in submitting a manuscript to the Aspatore editorial board, please email jason@aspatore.com with the book idea, your biography, and any additional pertinent information.

Inside the Minds:
The Ways of the VC

Leading Venture Capitalists on Identifying Opportunities, Assessing Business Models & Establishing Valuations

Contents

Acknowledgements & Dedications

On Making Investments and Working with Venture Capitalists

Graham Anderson

EuclidSR Partners
General Partner

Assessing an Investment Opportunity

There are three primary factors to examine when a venture capitalist assesses an investment opportunity. At the highest level of abstraction, they are the market, the management, and the exit opportunity.

As a firm, we are looking for very large, fast growing markets where small businesses can grow rapidly to become substantial enterprises within a relatively few years by capturing only a very small share of the overall market. We try to find opportunities that are relatively nascent and that address some unmet needs today but that will grow very rapidly in the near future. Our typical projected time horizon from investment to exit is three to five years for mid to later stage deals and five to seven years for earlier stage ones. We look for market sectors and business models that have fairly low barriers to entry today so that we can invest at a good price and then create escalating barriers to entry for the market of the future.

We look for management teams with the ability to execute on the plans that they have laid out, and the ability to make necessary changes when events do not go exactly as expected. As much as we would like it to be otherwise, the future does not follow a script. In many circumstances, keeping one's eye on the ball and focusing on the business plan can help prevent making costly mistakes due to overly zealous optimism about the potential for products and markets. In other situations, however, a team cannot be inflexible and stick to the plan at all costs; unfortunately, real life does not regularly play itself out like a business plan. Thus, teams have to be flexible and be able to make the changes necessary to have a successful venture.

Lastly, there have to be foreseeable exit opportunities so that the investors can realize a return on their investments. Although we are delighted when our portfolio companies are able to go public, no private investor can rely solely on the Initial Public Offering (IPO) market to make a return. Most exits are not IPOs. Moreover, to maximize the value of an investment, one cannot rely on a single buyer, in the absence of an IPO. To secure a good revenue or EBIT multiple upon a sale or to stimulate interest among buyers for a particular technology platform, a company must create multiple bidders in an exit scenario. From initial concept, a founder interested in venture financing must therefore create something that is valuable to many potential buyers. Nothing drives up a buyer's price like a competitor bidder trying to step in at the last minute and scoop up a prized asset. Ultimately, competitive bidding situations and the occasional IPO create the vast majority of venture returns.

Viewing an Opportunity from the Other Side of the Table

Not all good business opportunities are appropriate for venture funding. Plenty of very good businesses never receive venture capital. If an entrepreneur cannot envision an exit, then it is likely not an appropriate deal for a venture capitalist. Even in the best of times, venture capital is difficult to raise. Since the default answer to a request for money is always "No," it is best for an entrepreneur to remove as many obstacles to objections as possible before approaching sources of capital. For entrepreneurs, this means starting off on the right foot and never stumbling.

The most important first step is to secure a personal introduction to as many venture capital firms as one can. Getting in the door is one of the hardest things to do. When an entrepreneur is able to get that personal introduction, then he or she should have a skilled presenter help with the initial presentation so that it is in a format that is specifically tailored to the particular venture capital audience. The story needs to be very concise (venture capitalists are notorious for having short attention spans) and must lay out the roadmap to the money, the market and the management. An entrepreneur will typically only get one shot, so he or she really needs to be focused and persuasive.

Reducing the Risks that Venture Capitalists are Willing to Assume

In tough markets, investors are very unwilling to assume financing risk. As venture capitalists attempt to pull together syndicates of venture capital firms to invest in companies, we try to provide enough money around the boardroom table to see the company through an important milestone or to ultimate fruition by reaching either cash flow break, even on an operating basis or an exit event. Wherever possible, we are trying to change a company's risk profile by creating a syndicate that is strong enough from the beginning so that it takes away future financial risk in a new venture.

There are many risks that one cannot remove from deals, however. But it is important to remove or ameliorate as many as one can. Depending on the stage of the company, an investor may be willing to assume product risk. In every biotechnology company, without a marketed product, for example, there is product risk because there is no guaranty regarding what will happen at the Food and Drug Administration jury meetings, whose verdicts make or break products. Accordingly, as a firm, we would not typically invest in a single product company because the product risk (relying on a single New Drug Application) is simply too high. To be a biotech investor, however, means assuming some product risk in those types of companies. But as long as a company has a method of creating a pipeline of products behind a lead compound product, the product risk is diminished. Similarly, in software company deals, one always has market adoption risk. A few key, early-adopter customers, who will serve as product evangelists, help to reduce this risk. In addition, there may be some integration and technology risk, depending on how early in a company's lifecycle a venture capitalist invests. Generally, the more mature the company, the less product risk an investor takes.

The biggest risk investors assume, however, is management risk. Unfortunately, other than having a deep management bench, which is often too expensive for small companies, we have not found a complete solution to this problem. One cannot purchase management insurance. All a venture investor can do is take a board seat and participate in selecting upper management within the organization once the venture capitalist has made the investment. Even with rigorous interviewing, board members will still make some hiring mistakes.

Finding the Right People

When looking for management teams, a venture capitalist is looking for teams that have industry experience. They want business people who know the particulars of the markets in which they are operating. They are also looking for teams that can work in a small company environment. There are many very good executives who are excellent in Fortune 500 companies but who just do not make the transition to a small company environment, where they will need to make things happen with fewer resources at their disposal. Additionally, other than very senior managers at Fortune 500 companies who have had extensive rotations during long careers or veteran entrepreneurs, most CEOs making the transition to small companies will need to assume new roles that might be unfamiliar to them – from fundraising, to hiring and firing, to managing disparate departments within the small company, to handling external constituencies such as the media, customers, and potential partners. As an investor, one has to find the right members of an executive team who come from an entrepreneurial culture or who can readily adapt to a small company environment and its corresponding small-business mentality and responsibilities. Then, as the company succeeds and grows, the team must be flexible enough to grow out of its small company roots and into a larger organization with appropriate processes, checks and balances in its management structure.

Successful entrepreneurs understand the market, understand how to operate a small business, and understand that nobody is indispensable. A CEO must always backfill for employees so that the company will survive if anyone leaves. That single point is often the difference between success and failure in a startup.

A successful entrepreneur looks at his or her entire team and not just at a collection of individuals. The sum has to be greater than the parts. He or she hires people who realize that in a small company everyone is involved in sales. One cannot say "I just do finance" or "I'm only involved in engineering." That mentality is pernicious. Good startups have employees at all levels who know the market, who know the product, who know the customer, and who can sell the product. All those skills may not necessarily be in every person, but it is definitely in the culture of successful startups. It is preferable to have the gamut of these skills in a CEO, but it is not absolutely necessary. Nevertheless, a CEO who does not possess all of these skills must be introspective enough to recognize that fact so he or she can hire people who can bring such skills to the management of the company.

We look for entrepreneurs who truly understand the target market(s) that they are trying to enter and we try to ascertain how well they understand the dynamics, the competitive landscape, substitutable products, and so on. We delve into their assumptions and question whether they really understand in what areas their companies can compete effectively and efficiently. What is the company's true competitive advantage? Is the advantage sustainable? What is the core value proposition that the managers are offering? Do they articulate it well, precisely, quickly, and in a way that everyone can understand? If value cannot be understood very easily and very quickly to an audience that knows the market space, there is no way that the company will be able to make significant sales to its targeted customer base. Within a matter of minutes, companies seeking venture capital must be able to articulate their value proposition(s) to investors.

In the final analysis, we seek answers to the following questions: Are these individuals who can take a relatively small amount of money and execute according to their proposed plan? Do we believe that they can meet the goals and milestones that they have set out? If so, these fortunate entrepreneurs have a very good shot at being able to build a really great business.

Reaching an Appropriate Valuation

What many entrepreneurs frequently underestimate is where the risks inherently lie in their businesses, and how much capital is really necessary to build a substantial company. Moreover, entrepreneurs have a difficult time rationalizing an appropriate valuation that accurately reflects the true cost of capital. Frequently, they will not have chosen appropriate comparables or will have consulted a prestigious consulting firm that has crafted an elegant valuation analysis for them. When asked, "Is that firm going to write you a check at that valuation?," we know what the response will be. Although they are not perfectly efficient, supply and demand within the private equity markets determine appropriate valuations. Although entrepreneurs dwell inordinately on the question of valuation (What is my company worth?), it is much more productive to spend time on what they can get (other than money) from venture firms. Indeed, it is usually better to own 5 percent of California than 20 percent of Rhode Island.

For their limited partners, venture capitalists need to demonstrate a rate of return that is superior to what their investors can get in the public markets – because if they cannot do so, there is no point in taking the risk and illiquidity of investing in private equity. Appropriate discounts for risk and lack of liquidity can be very substantial. There are reasons why a company is not worth as much as an entrepreneur thinks it is worth, due to the various risks involved. And entrepreneurs need to have that undaunted optimism about their chances of success in order to be successful. Nevertheless, even though they too are optimists, venture capitalists must temper their optimism with pragmatism. It is important for an entrepreneur to understand what are the valuation parameters that a venture capitalist is considering – e.g. time to exit, amount of capital required, and interim financing valuations. Obviously, both sides try to get the best deal they can, but there is a limit to good negotiation. Beyond certain valuation points, (on the low end) entrepreneurs do not have sufficient incentive to perform and (on the high end) venture capitalists cannot get a venture return.

Determining the Market Size for a Venture-Backable Company

In terms of growth potential, venture capitalists look for deals that have the opportunity to be $100 million revenue businesses in five to ten years. Obviously, many companies do not end up getting there. Nevertheless, venture capitalists need to have "home run" opportunities in their portfolios so that a certain small percentage of the fund ends up being just that, blowout opportunities, and on the whole the portfolio does well. As a consequence, we look for the types of deals that have the potential for explosive, exponential growth rates.

A successful new business idea must be something that can be leveraged – that can take a relatively small amount of capital and turn it into something significant; if possible, a good deal should possess escalating barriers to entry and great opportunities for growth. Although there are a few exceptions, one of the businesses that is not typically appropriate for venture capital is consulting firms – the assets go down the elevator every night and it takes a huge number of bodies to be able to build them up. Other service-type businesses may be appropriate for venture capital, however. More typically, though, one sees product-oriented businesses backed by venture capitalists.

As a firm, we invest in three primary areas because they tend to be higher growth areas than the overall market: life sciences (predominately biotechnology), information technology (predominately software) and information services, and the overlap between those two markets. The convergence of information technology and life sciences is a very large growth area because health care firms have substantially under-invested in information technology over the past decade or more. There are other vertical markets that can also produce very successful venture investments. Specialty, retail is one. Telecommunications, when that market roars back, will be another. There are many other areas that have the economics and the potential to have blowout deals, but not every venture capital firm invests in every sector. Indeed, many are industry- or geography-specific funds.

Understanding the Cyclical Nature of Private Equity

Markets go up. Markets go down. The same story plays itself out in private markets as well as public ones. And when markets remain down for extended periods, one begins to see significant consolidation in various market sectors.

Over the past few years, one of the trends we have noticed is merger opportunities among companies within venture capitalists' portfolios. Thus far, we have seen this phenomenon played out more aggressively on the information technology side of our business than on the biotechnology side, but we believe this situation may change and encompass biotech firms in the not-too-distant future. During difficult market times, venture capital investors try to pull together and pool resources among their companies so that the surviving entities end up having a much higher opportunity for success. One of the reasons venture capitalists are acting so impatiently is that in down-markets capital becomes exceedingly expensive – and after the bubble years of the late 1990s, we are experiencing as high a cost of capital as our industry has witnessed since its very early days. When there are no real IPO or secondary markets, the cost of capital skyrockets, and even good companies find that the cost of capital from new venture investors is prohibitively expensive. Instead, they seek to gain access to capital and grow via mergers and acquisitions.

Raising Venture Capital

Raising money is a lot of work. And it is important for entrepreneurs not to waste time soliciting investors who are not likely to make an investment. Time is precious and is better off spent in front of potential customers or partners. An entrepreneur has to figure out whether venture capital is appropriate for his or her business. It is not appropriate for every type of business. An entrepreneur's target market sector may not be big enough for venture capitalists, even if it may be a very good business for the entrepreneur. Once a founder decides that venture capital is accessible, then he or she must determine whether the targeted venture capital firms do early stage investing. Many venture capital firms focus on later stage deals.

Moreover, an entrepreneur must ascertain whether the venture capital firm specializes in making investments in the entrepreneur's industry or in the appropriate geography. For example, a firm might focus exclusively on telecommunications investments and only on those investments in the northeastern United States. If an entrepreneur expects to get the kind of sales and business development support that he or she wants and needs from a venture capitalist who is going to be on the company's board, then one needs to go after venture capital firms in proximity to the company. For more mature companies, however, proximity does not matter nearly as much.

After ascertaining whether the venture firm is an appropriate capital source and a good industry, stage and geographic match, the entrepreneur then needs to determine how much capital is required to build the business and what amount the venture capital firm is capable of deploying towards the investment. In addition, the CEO of the venture should ask the firm's general partners whether they prefer to lead deals or participate in a syndicate; in challenging times, it is critical to find a lead investor willing to put a stake in the ground and a number on a term sheet. Most importantly, for the relationship to be successful, the entrepreneur must feel comfortable working with the venture capitalists and like their approach to venture investing. The entrepreneur should seek venture capital firms that bring compatible investment and operational philosophies into the boardroom. In other words, the entrepreneur and the venture capitalist must be aligned with one another in terms of what they both want to get out of the relationship.

Before signing any definitive legal documents with a venture capital firm, an entrepreneur should speak with other management teams with whom the venture capital firm has invested. He or she should interview the participants involved with both the success stories and the less-than-successful ventures to determine what it was like to work with the venture capital firm when events did not turn out as planned. Such a process is particularly important to assess how the partners were able to add value, and how they were able to adjust plans to do whatever was necessary to make the venture a successful business, even though it did not look like it was going to be very successful.

Navigating Due Diligence

For early stage enterprises, the most important part of due diligence is getting to know the management team – trying to walk in their shoes, spending significant time with them, and figuring out whether or not this is the team that can actually drive the business forward.

On the product side, investors must believe in the long-term viability and size of the market and understand it as well as the entrepreneurs do. We will conduct market research independent of what entrepreneurs have done. We will speak with actual and potential customers and become engaged in the market ourselves whenever possible.

If a new deal involves a specific technology with which we are relatively unfamiliar, we, along with many other firms, will engage consultants to help us take a look at it. We will sometimes ask our current portfolio companies to take a look at a novel technology for us as well and offer their opinions. Within the time constraints that we feel are appropriate for the specific deal, we will do as much as we can to understand: 1) the market that the company is attacking; 2) the product's position within its specific niche; and 3) the product's "fit" and potential extensions into the broader market beyond the company's initial targets. Finally, we attempt to determine whether our strategic visions are aligned with the management's. If so, we have uncovered a really promising opportunity for investment.

Surviving Due Diligence

With regard to surviving venture capital due diligence, a management team will basically be asked to provide as much information as it can. Although it is best to keep the initial meeting short and sweet and an initial presentation targeted to a typical *Wall Street Journal* or *Economist* reader, it is almost impossible to provide too much detail as a deal graduates from the "meet and greet" phase to more intense due diligence. Since investors are continually looking for reasons to move on to the next opportunity and the deals that get done are the ones that possess the fewest red flags, management should be capable of backing up every data point with independent research and provide as many references as possible. The entrepreneur should try to work closely with his or her own advisors – accountants, lawyers, and consultants – to make all presentations and records look as neat, clean, polished and professional as possible when presenting to venture capitalists. Under the close eye of scrutiny, venture capitalists are always looking for red flags.

Some red flags include: gaps in managers' employment histories, unusual choices of references, insufficient or obscure backup data for claims regarding market size, or less than stellar reference customers (or a failure to have asked customers in advance to provide references). If entrepreneurs have financial projections that they cannot support with primary and third party research, they will have a hard time closing a financing.

Working with Venture Capitalists

A venture capitalist's primary function on a portfolio company's board is to represent the shareholders – and often most specifically the shareholders in the class of stock in which the venture firm has invested. An entrepreneur should not forget that first and foremost a venture investor owes a fiduciary duty to his or her limited and general partners. Investors may love their companies, but they will not fall on their swords for them. As a practical matter, venture investors do not typically manage a company's day-to-day affairs. Nevertheless, venture capitalists may serve very effectively as ancillary sales, business development and strategy team members for their portfolio companies. Whenever possible, venture capitalists will "knock on doors," make introductions, generate leads, recruit employees and help a company raise money. When it comes down to the final analysis, however, a venture investor's role is basically to decide whether or not the current CEO is the person to run that company for the future.

Because by their very nature, they (and the entrepreneurs) are eternal optimists, venture capitalists will rarely replace underperforming management teams quickly. Frequently, the investors believe strongly in the people that they have backed and almost always wait too long to make necessary management changes. In our firm's experience, almost all unsuccessful venture capital investments arise from management failures and the reluctance to replace underperforming managers quickly. Although one will sometimes find that a company fails because its product was too far ahead of its market, actual product failures or fraud are very rare.

Closing a Deal and Managing Investors

From an entrepreneur's perspective, we believe it is advisable to choose a syndicated deal with several venture capital investors whenever possible; in a typical venture deal, a CEO should avoid being beholden to a single investor. Indeed, an entrepreneur will want to have the opportunity to go to separate people for board and investor level assistance. In our opinion, in a small syndicate the rewards of having multiple parties work for a company outweigh the risk of conflicting views held by multiple investors. And we feel the benefits from multiple relationships also outweigh the rewards of dealing with a single investor. In a syndicate, an entrepreneur will have more lead generation, more sales assistance, and more strategic thinking with a broader base of opinions from different venture firms. One can go too far and be overly syndicated, however, and then there is risk in not being able to manage all of the investors. In general, it is much better to rely on a small syndicate than to be beholden to one investor, and a large syndicate is sometimes preferable to no syndicate at all.

Above all, the entrepreneur needs to manage investor expectations. One of the most frequent mistakes that tends to trip up entrepreneurs is over-promising and under-delivering results. It is a natural mistake as the skill set necessary to become an entrepreneur rarely leads to the perspective necessary to manage long-term investor relations. When an entrepreneur overcomes this quandary, the sky is the limit. An open line of communication between investors and portfolio companies is the key to a successful long-term relationship.

Graham Anderson is a General Partner with EuclidSR Partners, an early-stage venture capital firm with over $250 million under management in its current fund and offices in New York City and the greater Philadelphia area.

Prior to joining EuclidSR, Mr. Anderson served in several professional capacities in management consulting, law, software and new media. Mr. Anderson comes to EuclidSR Partners from the strategy consulting firm, Salzinger & Company, a division of CommerceOne (NASDAQ: CMRC). At Salzinger & Co., Mr. Anderson served as a consultant to America Online's Greenhouse Project, Image Technology Corporation (now network MCI Digital Imaging), CI Impressions, Inc., and The Walt Disney Company. Prior to joining Salzinger & Company, Mr. Anderson practiced law at Susman Godfrey L.L.P. in Houston where he concentrated on securities, private equity and software law. Mr. Anderson is a CFA Charterholder and a graduate of Yale College, the University of Glasgow and the Yale Law School.

Mr. Anderson serves on the Editorial Advisory Board of VentureOne, the Board of Directors of the Venture Industry Association of New York (VIANY), chairs the Technology Showcase Conference sponsored by the New York New Media Association and is an active participant in software and information industry organizations with an emphasis on the convergence of information technologies and life sciences. Mr. Anderson concentrates on enterprise software, convergence of information technology and life sciences and specialty pharmaceutical investing. Mr. Anderson serves on the boards of directors of several private companies.

Venture Capital Today:

May You Live In Interesting Times

Oliver D. Curme

Battery Ventures
General Partner

Adapting to Change

Interesting times for an even more interesting industry. Over the past five years, the venture capital industry has seen and lived through the best and the worst of times. It's been a painful series of reality adjustments as venture capitalists have had to adapt to a financial and IT market environment that has completely changed since 1999. From setting valuations and assessing risk to who you have relationships with and how you work with and support the companies you make investments in, the landscape has changed. The venture capitalists who will survive are the ones who accept these changes and adapt their business practices to today's new economic realities. In this chapter we will discuss all of these issues to provide a picture of how the venture capital market looks today as well as what the future holds.

Company Valuation

The traditional wisdom regarding venture capital deals is that there are three components to value: management, management, management. At Battery Ventures, we take a very different approach, however. We think there are three determinants of value in a company and those are market, market, and market. To give an example, compare the current environment to the bubble in 1998-1999-2000. In a great market like that, when pigs could fly and you could sell just about anything to anybody, even idiots got rich. In a tough market like we have today, where companies are cutting way back on capital spending and they're not buying from young software companies, it's very hard even for superman management teams to stay alive. So the biggest determinant of value, I believe, is having the right product at the right time in the right market. There are other ingredients: management – yes, it is important, the financial plan and exit, and the product and technology. If you analyze the market, market barriers and competitive differentiation are clearly important, but the most crucial issue, by which you're going to win or lose, is the product market environment: whether customers really want to buy a lot of what the company is selling.

Generally, a company's valuation can be set by the market. That's the way prices are set in a capitalist society: by supply and demand. So when an entrepreneur goes out to get financing, he needs to expose the opportunity to enough qualified investors to get a diversity of thoughts on price, and hopefully within that diversity there will be what he sees as a fair price. If an entrepreneur thinks his company is worth a hundred million dollars and all the venture capitalists are telling him it's worth ten million dollars – well, the venture capital valuation has been set at ten million, not a hundred million. So the valuation process for entrepreneurs, simply, boils down to taking the opportunity to a sufficient number of good quality investors.

On the other hand, from my point of view the correct value of a company is the lowest value I can get, at least within limits. I don't ever want to take all of the company and demotivate the employees and the management team. But as a venture capitalist, my job is to buy low and sell high. My job is not to set a fair price, but to find those unusual opportunities where I can get the best price, or an unusual price. It's like buying a house; you want to find a motivated seller and someone who didn't take it to a lot of different buyers. We usually don't find un-shopped deals; most opportunities are presented to our competition. In those cases, we generally establish what we think is the maximum value, and we'll walk away from a deal if we don't see an expected case return between three and five times our investment.

What makes venture capitalists different from other professionals valuing companies is that ours is a less liquid market. It's more like real estate – or it's even less liquid than real estate. In the stock market, you've got thousands of people setting the price, and in private equity, if you've got half a dozen interested buyers, you're probably lucky. The other way to look at it is that the outcomes in private equity have a huge dispersion. If you buy a stock, it's probably going to trade like most of the other stocks. You might get lucky and it might double or triple, or you might get unlucky and the company might go bankrupt, but most stocks travel together. That's not the case with private equity companies. With venture-capital-backed companies, the rule of thumb is that 20 to 30 percent of the companies provide the bulk of the returns in a venture capital portfolio. And sometimes it's one or two companies in a portfolio that provide almost all the returns. There's a huge variation in outcome, and the winners are what keeps this business exciting.

Risk Assessment

Venture capitalists have to be able to tolerate, analyze, and manage risk better than most public stock managers. If you ignore the management of risk, venture capital is similar to managing other illiquid pools of investment, such as hedge funds, arbitrage, or junk bonds. But for the most part, venture capitalists are dealing with riskier individual investments. However, there's an interesting paradox in that while most people perceive venture capital funds as risky, the funds themselves are probably less risky and less volatile than most other investment segments. This is something most people don't realize. It's due to the portfolio effect: even with risky startup companies that could either go to the moon or crash, if you aggregate ten or fifteen of them, the law of averages smoothes out the returns. You still deal with systemic risk, if your venture portfolio is concentrated in a certain market, but the beauty of venture portfolios is that you can average out all the individual risks inherent in early stage companies.

We like to see a minimum of three to five times return on our investment. As contrasted with most other money managers, we're more geared toward return multiples than internal rates of return. And the reason for that is that the internal rate of return – which is the way most equity or bond funds are measured – looks toward annualized returns on a portfolio year after year after year. With a venture capital portfolio, we're trying to invest in a variety of companies and make as much of a multiple as we can, and if it takes two or three years longer to return five times the fund, that's fine with us. We don't care if it takes longer to get an exit, as long as we're generating aggregate returns of 25 or 30 percent annualized, because those aggregate returns greatly outweigh returns in the public markets. That's a very significant trait of venture capitalists: we're capital patient. We raise funds with ten year lives and often extensions to twelve or thirteen years. So we can afford to spend the time to work with companies over long periods of times if those companies are going to return three times our invested capital, or five, or ten, or in some cases fifty or a hundred.

To determine which risks are worth taking, we do a Monte Carlo analysis on all of our proposed deals: we look at the upside, at the expected case, at a conservative case and a worst case. So our return models are somewhat skewed toward the conservative side, and the worst-case scenario is almost always that you lose all your money because you could almost always lose all your money. When you go through the process of putting together that sort of analysis that really sketches out the risk-return parameters of a deal. Is this a one in ten chance of making a huge return, or is this a fairly consistent company with a fairly predictable return outcome? Is it very risky or less risky? We're OK with really risky deals if the upside is there. We're OK with deals that have relatively little risk as long as we can make three times our money. Between those two extremes, there are no real metrics; it's just your gut feel, it's the environment, and it's working with your partners and seeing what opportunities they have, and picking the best opportunities in that environment on a subjective basis.

Investment Relationships

Even though the product market is the biggest determinant of value, we won't do a deal unless we can work with the management team. That doesn't mean that the whole management team has to be in place. In fact, I would say at least half of our deals are companies with a founder and very little management team. We spend a lot of time helping companies recruit great talent in the sales area, in marketing, in R&D, and eventually in the CFO role. So we help companies fill out their management team. We'll start with just one founder, but the criteria for the people we hire, as well as that founder, are that they have to have strong ethics, they have to really know their business or know the market segment they're in. The management also has to want to work with us as a partner – because we're an active venture firm and we roll up our sleeves and work with the team. If someone is just looking for money, they'd probably find it at a better price somewhere else.

A venture capital investment can be in place for many years. Even though this is a deal-oriented business, you don't live or die by the terms of those deals. It's counterproductive to try to squeeze every nickel out of the other side. What's important is the long-term relationship you have with the management team. Back in the bubble, we may have overpaid for deals. And now, back in this environment, maybe entrepreneurs are giving up too much of their companies. Maybe valuations are too low. But it will even out. A great man, Simon Ramo, taught me that lesson when I invested in one of my first deals, HNC Software. In three years, if the company is doing really well and the environment is pretty good, those founders are going to go back to the board and say, "We need more stock options," and their ownership will come to a fair level over a long period of time. It's important not to get all riled up over the detailed complexities of a particular deal and just focus on building value and building relationships for the long run.

I think the same thing applies to entrepreneurs. In fact, it's more difficult for the entrepreneurs to take that point of view, because whereas the VC firm might do ten or twenty deals a year, an entrepreneur is maybe going to do one deal every three to five years, so that deal is much more important to him (or her). But again, look beyond the term sheet and don't go for the deal with the best terms. Go for the partner that you think is going to add the most value and is going to be the best to work with for a long period of time. In some sense, it's like a marriage, and you've got to pick a partner that's going to be there in good times and bad, not just the latest guy who drove up in a flashy car and threw down the best terms on a term sheet.

Finding the Right Investment Opportunities

Analyzing the market for a product is where all the work comes in. It is easiest when we find a big established market that's undergoing a huge transformation or dislocation due to the introduction of new technology. That doesn't mean that our companies all sell technology per se, but they all tend to be in markets that are being transformed by the adoption of some kind of technology. For example, I was in Chicago a number of years ago and we had some free time, so we decided to visit with a friend who walked us down to see the Chicago Board of Trade. It was an eye-opening experience for me. I stood on an observation platform and looked out on a sea of a few thousand people down in the trading pits, all wearing brightly colored jackets, all screaming at the top of their lungs and gesticulating with funny sign language. I stood up there and I said to my partner, Scott Tobin, "This is Dickensian! This is the sort of thing I know my children won't see, because this sort of human pit trading, open market trading – which is how stock markets got established hundreds of years ago – is going to be replaced by a computer. I just know it." And that launched us on a project where we explored how technology would impact the futures market, because many other markets, such as the stock market, are pretty much fully automated. The futures market is still almost completely traded by people in the pits.

It took us more than two years of study looking at lots of different investment opportunities, before we found an investment in the London Financial Futures Exchange (LIFFE), which is a futures exchange that trades financial futures – foreign exchange and the Pound futures. We found this deal in London at a point when they had just finished developing a computerized trading system and had converted their entire floor, with thousands of traders, to software running in a box. We decided to invest in the exchange to help them take their system worldwide. LIFFE introduced stock futures with our help; they spread their technology to the States (with NASDAQ) and also to Japan. They grew very quickly. In a little over a year we sold the company to another

European futures exchange which was consolidating the business, and we made a very handsome return. The point of this story is that we looked first at a market that we thought was going to undergo a huge transformation, and then we looked around at the different ways to play that market. Some were software companies, some were hardware companies, and some were communications companies. We finally ended up investing in a futures exchange itself, which on the surface might not sound like a venture deal, but it had all the components of market dislocation and technology that led to a great return, and that's generally how we make our money.

It's not easy to spend two and a half years researching a market before you actually make an investment. It is easier at our firm because we're overstaffed. We have more than thirty investment professionals, which is a lot for a venture capital firm that makes twelve to fifteen new deals per year. We're comprised of ten general partners, with younger associates and senior associates, who are very smart, hard-working men and women, typically in their twenties and thirties. We form teams of three people who will work on a project together. It's a mentoring symbiosis: the experienced general partners have lots of experience but very little time; their time is valuable. And the younger people have plenty of time but not experience. Venture capital is one of the last apprenticeship trades, but years of hands-on training is needed in order to learn all the aspects of our craft. In fact, almost all of our general partners started out as young associates and grew up through the ranks in that mentoring fashion. Our project approach has been crucial for building a strong team culture and a leveraged organization, with a lot of human resources that we can throw at projects.

Ego is a big red flag when we're considering an investment. The people we're looking to back are people who want to build a company. Many entrepreneurs are looking to build their resume, or looking to build a kingdom that they can control. So we're looking for people who are headstrong enough to be entrepreneurs (you've got to be pretty headstrong to be an entrepreneur), but also open enough to realize that the company is not going to be defined by the founder. The company is going to be successful if they recruit a broad team; the company is going to transcend the founder. So ego issues are crucial. While it's clear we can work with some people, others don't want to hear anything unless it fits with their ego.

Let me give an example of how this works. There's a crucial discussion that needs to take place between the investors and management team prior to the investment. It's the "What if things don't work out?" discussion. It's easy to look at a business plan, and say, "Oh, great. If this goes to the moon, we'll all make a lot of money. This looks like fun. Let's invest." But what if it doesn't work? What if things do not go as planned? What if, in the first six months, we don't sell any of this? Then what are we going to do? The founder is smart if he has that conversation before the venture capitalist invests than after the end of those six months. Because it's through the scenario discussions of what could go wrong, and what you would do if that went wrong, that the venture capitalist will understand the flexibility of the entrepreneur, and the entrepreneur will understand the flexibility of the venture capitalist. Nothing ever goes exactly as planned. It never does. Sometimes it's better; sometimes it's worse. So people really need to focus on the variability in the plan and on people's different expectations of what should happen.

Tips for Entrepreneurs

Frankly, many entrepreneurs don't know how to approach venture firms, so here are some tips:

1) Don't go to too many venture firms, and don't go to too few. Go to enough venture firms so that you'll be exposed to a number of good investors, and see what happens. If you go to half a dozen highly qualified venture capital firms who are investing in your area, that's probably enough to test the waters. If you go to 100 firms, few will take you seriously because they'll think you don't know how to raise money.

2) Ask for feedback! If you talk to six qualified investors and they're not interested, you need to find out why. I almost never have a management team ask us our opinion after a presentation. We throw out all these questions to the entrepreneurs, and they never turn around and say, "Well, what do you think about this? How does this compare to other things you're looking at? What are the strengths of our deal? What are the weaknesses? How could we change this opportunity so it would fit your investment criteria?"

3) Target the right firms. There are many people who approach me with biotech plans, and we don't do any biotech. It's not in our charter. If they'd done their homework and gone to our website, they would have known that we don't make investments in their market. But they waste a lot of time trying to get to me and set up a meeting to pitch me on a deal we would never do. So entrepreneurs should do their homework to find the most likely investor, and not just blanket every VC in some directory with a business plan. Now, how do you do that? If you have a company doing a next generation video conferencing system, the best way to find

an investor is to look at the last generation of video conferencing systems and see who invested in those deals. If you have a video conferencing startup, go back and research who invested in PictureTel. Because if a venture capitalist invested in PictureTel, not only did they learn the industry, but they made a lot of money, so they'll be favorably disposed to investing in the sector again. So you need to qualify the venture firm as one that has already invested in the sector and hopefully made a lot of money. Those are the best prospects. And the way to do that is to look back through history, find the closest comparable successful companies, and find who the investors were.

4) Personal references are the next step. Once you determine that you want to get in to see us, you have to recognize that we see about 10,000 business plans a year. We have a big staff, but we're also getting a lot of mailbags in every day with unsolicited business plans. It's a relationship business, and the best way to approach a venture firm is to network in. Personal introductions wouldn't matter in a perfect world because we'd spend a lot of time on every deal to really dig through it, but I would say roughly half the deals we eventually do come through a personal introduction, and the other half are either ones that come across the transom or ones that we go out into the marketplace and find ourselves, and we approach them instead of them approaching us.

5) Your first meeting should facilitate building a relationship. The worst presentations are the ones where I get in the conference room and someone has a 100-slide PowerPoint presentation that's completely memorized and that they insist on drilling through in rapid fashion. That's not really conducive to a relationship. I would much rather sit across the table with a small number of slides and walk through asking questions and getting into discussion with that person, rather than

hearing some sort of static, force-fed presentation. The way I like to start a meeting is by asking the entrepreneur to tell me about his background. How did you get here? What were the factors that led you to get into this business? History's important, and that often brings lots of interesting insights into the discussion. It can demonstrate the entrepreneur's credibility and knowledge, which is very important. And if the VC is not asking questions, ask him questions: "Here's our sales strategy; this is how we think we should approach sales. What do you think? What other sales strategies have you seen from other companies in this business?" Or: "How does this compare to other deals in your portfolio? How does this compare to other deals you've seen in this market? What do you think are our strengths and weaknesses?" And when the meeting is over: "What's the next step? Where do we go from here? What did you like about this? What don't you like about this? If you're not interested in investing, who do you know that might be a better prospect?"

Board Participation

Our philosophy at Battery is to be active board members, to the point where sometimes we'll take two board seats. We lead most of our deals, and we're often the only investor in the company, so we have to play a pretty active role. We don't rely heavily on other syndicate partners to do all the work. That's called "value-added." If you ask any venture capitalist, "Are you going to add a lot of value? Are you going to help out the company?" They all say yes. Everyone says, "Oh, yes. We'll add more value to your company than any other venture capital firm." Now, the problem is that some are not entirely truthful. Entrepreneurs need to do their homework to figure out who really is going to add value and who isn't. They need to find out who is going to be on that board of directors. It's a relationship not just with a venture firm, but more importantly, with that investment professional at that firm. And then you have to find out what other boards that person is on. And how many boards is that person on? At our firm, we're on an average of four boards per investment professional, so we try to keep the workload manageable. In some firms, it gets up to twelve or sixteen boards, and it's very hard for any investment professional to spend time with a company if they're on twelve or sixteen boards.

Board references are another area where entrepreneurs need to do their homework. Not only should they ask what other boards the VC is on, they should call the CEOs of those other companies and say, "What is this guy like to work with? What value have they added to your company?" It's amazing that we always do extensive reference checking, and the companies we're investing in almost never ask. We have to volunteer. We give these companies a sheet of our CEOs with names and numbers and say, "Call these guys, because that's the only way you'll really know what we're like to work with, in good times and in bad times."

Do venture capitalists add value, and if so, where? I think venture capitalists can add value in four different areas. The first is recruiting. The management team of the company doesn't recruit as much as the venture capitalists. We're always in the market for talent. We're the best-paid recruiters in the world. We've got big contact networks; we can really help find the best CEO, sales, R&D, and marketing talent, as well as board members. Recruiting is always important. Some entrepreneurs might say, "I've got a full team, so I don't need to care about recruiting." That's not true. If you're successful, you're going to be overseas in no time. You're going to be doing acquisitions. The best companies grow fast, and fast growing companies always have a scarcity of talent. So recruiting is number one.

The second issue is strategic help. That's a combination of helping companies with their strategies – with their marketing strategies, their sales strategies, and competitive dynamics – as well as introducing them to strategic partners. Flying at 60,000 feet, we see a lot of companies pursue a lot of different sales, marketing, development, and strategic partnering strategies, so it's a legitimate area for us to share our experiences. And given the reach of contacts that we have within portfolio companies and beyond, we can often help with partner introductions. Especially nowadays, when it's very hard for a young company to sell into a Fortune 500 company. A high level venture introduction to a great channel partner, a company like IBM, for example, can often help a company fly across the early stage chasm.

The third one is financial. When an entrepreneur partners with a venture firm, the VC firm should take over the investment banking function for that company. They should help the company raise the next round, broaden the syndicate, get investments from strategic partners, prepare for going public, or help negotiate a merger or sale. Again, that's something we do all the time. We've done it in hundreds of portfolio companies, and it's something that portfolio companies don't do that often, so it makes sense for the venture board member to really take a lead role there.

The final area of value add is a marketing/PR function that I call "buzz." There are lots and lots of venture-funded companies out there. There are, by some accounts more than 10,000 companies that were funded during the bubble that are still alive. It's really hard for a little company to get its head above water and to get noticed, and to get placement on the cover of industry trade magazines, to get mentioned in *The Wall Street Journal*, to really create a buzz around that company so that it seems a lot bigger than it really is. A venture capitalist can't always help in that regard, but the best ones, who have good contacts, can really help drive the excitement and public perception and buzz around a company; that can really help it stand out in a crowded market. Think how Kleiner Perkins helped drive the buzz around Ginger/Segway!

Syndicates

At Battery we usually lead our deals. We're the first institutional investor in most of the companies we invest in, so we don't typically go into deals where there are already five or six venture capital firms in a deal. That can be a real recipe for disaster, because venture capitalists don't always think alike. There is nothing as frustrating as a company, gridlocked because it has too many venture capitalists pulling in different directions. So if we bring syndicate partners into a deal, we like them to add something that we're lacking. For example, we often have market experts who really know a particular market in the software communications segment. If we're investing in a company in a certain geographical area, we'll often want to augment our expertise with a regional venture capitalist, because they might have a lot of local contacts we don't have. It's important when you look at venture capital syndicates that, (a) they are not too big, and (b) they are complementary to each other. You don't want identical twins of two different venture firms that always co-invest together and always think alike. You want to bring some different perspective to the table.

The other important thing in building boards goes beyond the venture capitalists. It's very important to get independent investors, or independent board members, on a board. We often build balanced boards where a third of the board seats are management and founders, a third are venture capitalists, and a third are outsiders. On a six-member board, that would be two and two and two. We want it to be a balanced relationship, with no one constituency dominating the others. It's hard to get really great independent board members, especially these days, with Sarbanes/Oxley and lots of personal litigation exposure from serving on boards. But it's possible if it's an exciting opportunity – and often it's an industry heavyweight who may have sold his company and wants to give back by mentoring a younger CEO. Building a balanced board with good independent board members is not easy, but it's a critical part of having a really strong functioning board.

Changes and Trends in Investment Strategies

In some ways, investment strategy has changed dramatically in the last few years. The environment has certainly changed. Again, venture capitalists lie. You'll ask people if they got caught up during the bubble, and they'll say, "Oh, no. We didn't do any stupid deals during the bubble. Everybody else did those deals but not us." Unfortunately, almost everybody got carried away in the bubble due to the get-rich-quick opportunities, and because the public markets were valuing concept companies in the billions of dollars of valuation. Like many other firms during the bubble, we concentrated on building new concept companies. Fortunately, the market's gotten more rational. It was fun, but it was unreal and a little crazy back during the bubble, and now we're back to a Darwinian survival of the fittest environment, which is an appropriate way to deploy capital intelligently and effectively. We're back to being agents of the invisible hand of capitalism as opposed to the drunken hand of capitalism. Right now, only the best deals get financing, and only the strongest and the best companies survive. It's a jungle out there, but that's probably the way it should be. There was too much money being spent too freely during the bubble.

Comparing investments today versus four years ago, valuations are way down. The deals that we are seeing tend to be much higher quality; they're often well thought out, with strong business models. If they're selling products to large companies, the products generally have a very strong return-on-investment opportunity for the buyer – very fast payback often in just a few months for the price of the product. So the quality of the deals we're seeing has gone up, and the valuations have come down. That's good.

Another thing that's changed is that companies are being run today in a much more cash-efficient manner than four years ago. Today it's good to conserve cash. It used to be the bigger the burn rate, the better. Today, since you're unlikely to sell a company or take it public for much more than $200 million, you can't really invest $50 million in a company and have an adequate return, so we're focusing on cash efficiency where people are doing it the old way. They're getting a company up and started on maybe $5 million or $10 million in capital as opposed to $30 million or $50 million in capital. Companies are being run much more tightly. They're getting a lot more customer funding than they did during the bubble. We're back to seeing application software companies develop their product by selling a custom job to one firm, then a custom job to the next, and slowly refining their product over the course of three or four custom jobs, which they get paid for – a more rational development process than raising a lot of money, building a huge development team, and working away for 24 months.

We are looking at more later-stage opportunities these days. Four years ago, there weren't any later-stage opportunities. Four years ago, everything was early stage, even public companies. Today, we're seeing opportunities to spin out a $50 million division of a larger company, or to invest in a public company that has $50 million in recurring revenues at incredibly low valuations. We're a balanced fund, and we'll go later-stage when the risk-return profile of those deals is attractive. Right now, it's much more compelling to invest in a company that has tens of millions of revenue, a strong customer base, and strong recurring revenue than a startup. Because often the valuations are exactly the same.

The Future of Venture Capital

We seem to be at a crossroads. We all knew we were in a bubble that couldn't last, but even that foreknowledge didn't soften the bumpy ride we've had since the bubble burst in spring of 2000. It has been a painful series of reality adjustments to adapt to a financial and IT market environment which now is completely reversed from that of 1999. Are we at the bottom? When will the turnaround happen? Will the turnaround happen? What does the future hold?

I have no idea what exactly is going to happen. No one could have forecasted September 11, war in Iraq, or that half of the ten largest corporate bankruptcies[1] in history would happen in 2002. But although I don't know what exactly will happen, as a venture capitalist I am forced

---

[1]http://www.businessweek.com/bwdaily/dnflash/jan2003/nf2003012_8278.htm

to forecast trends. It's my job. Venture capital is divination, forecasting the direction of economic, societal and technical trends so that we can get out in front of big trends, back high potential businesses and make a lot of money for our investors. Venture Capital is contrarian; you have to spot the big trend before the next guy. Once everyone sees what's going on, everyone can jump in the game and it will be hard for a little company to take on all comers. By now everyone knows the potential of ecommerce software, search engines, J2EE development tools and CRM software, and it's damn difficult for a new company to get in there and elbow out everyone else to become dominant. The ecosystem of Information Technology (IT) is well colonized with all manner of well adapted, hungry and savage companies. It's a jungle out there.

Show Me the Opportunities

So where are the NEW opportunities? What's the next really big thing? That's what all the VC's are wondering (while thousands of dying companies are asking Where's the money?)[2] Since 1980 we've had a great run of whopper IT trends: the PC, workstation, "Packaged" Enterprise Software, Client Server, Databases, LANs, and the mother of all trends, the Internet. OK, what's next? What's the next big trend that no one sees? Well? How about nothing? What if there wasn't one?

---

[2] http://www.content.loudeye.com/scripts/hurlPNM.exe?/~oo-600005/0118527_0103_00_0002.ra

Moore's Curse

We all know Moore's law.[3] It states that the density of computer chips doubles every eighteen months and so far it has held true for eighteen generations, since 1965. And since chip costs are directly proportional to area, chip costs have fallen by 99.988 percent over the past twenty years. Fortunately the tech markets have been price elastic. As computers and storage got cheaper, new applications were invented in a virtuous spiral of invention and automation which has been the engine of our economic growth over the past twenty years.

The assumption is that this virtuous invention spiral continues forever. But nothing goes on forever. You can't keep doubling forever,[4] or, more to the point, even if you could, who cares? At some point the price elasticity of IT markets may stop. Computers will be fast enough. You'll have enough storage. And when that happens, markets stop growing and start shrinking. Thus I formulate Moore's Curse:

Despite continued price declines in technology, at some point price elasticity in certain IT markets will stop, and market growth will be replaced by deflationary market shrinkage.

---

[3] http://www.intel.com/update/archive/issue2/feature.htm
[4] http://www.touchnet.com/cci/02.htm

Let's take an example. Computer disk drives have had 40 percent annual price/bit declines[5] over the past several years. Today you can buy an 80GB disk drive for $130[6]. In five years, you'll be able to buy a 1 Terabyte drive for $130. What can you do with 1 Terabyte? Aha, we all know the answer: Video! The storage and transport demand will be insatiable! According to Moore's Curse, nothing is insatiable. There are even limits to video! You can't watch video for much more than twelve hours per day. At 50 cents per hour of video (or 4 cents in ten years) who needs a lot more storage for video?

All Good Things Come to an End

The wave of IT innovation has been so big and its prosperity so dramatic, that forecasting an eventual end to it is heresy. You need to look at longer periods of history to see the analogous events. History is filled with examples of precious commodities, which drove economies until man figured out how to make enough. The backbone of the early Celtic economies was salt[7]. Now who cares about salt? Until the agricultural revolution of the last two centuries, food was the most precious commodity. Now, at least in the US, we have enough and its cost is almost incidental.

---

[5] http://query.nytimes.com/gst/abstract.html?res=F0081FFD345A0C718DDDA8 0894DB404482
[6] http://www.pcconnection.com/scripts/productdetail.asp?product_id=287763
[7] http://cynthia.spindler.fr/builth/History/Celts.htm

Economic trends do not run straight; they come in waves as societies evolve. Capital markets respond by allocating capital to businesses that drive progress, satisfying existing needs at lower costs. If progress is especially rapid, this can lead to investment cycles of boom and bust, such as railroads and mining in the late nineteenth century, automotive in the 1920's and 1930's, and the electronics IPO boom and bust in the 1960's.

I think the huge boom we've had in the Information Technology business is over; the industry has matured. Corporate Information Technology isn't going away, but growth has flattened. There will continue to be innovation and small nimble companies will displace big slow ones and money will be made. But without overall sector growth, there will be much less wealth creation, and the frequency of success stories will be greatly diminished. The following chart shows US Information Technology spending as a percentage of all business capital investment. As you can see, this number has increased tenfold since 1950. It is unlikely to even double again.

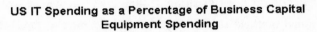

US IT Spending as a Percentage of Business Capital Equipment Spending

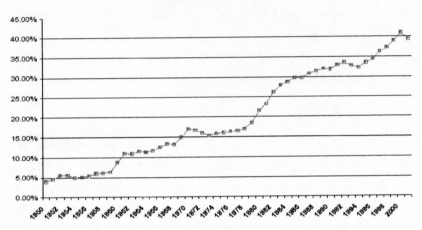

Source: US Dept of Commerce

This is not just my own conclusion. Ben Howe, at SG Cowen says that "a combination of economic, market, and technological factors will limit secular growth for the IT industry to a mid-single digit pace," and that investors ought to "get used to it." Another conclusion from SG Cowen is that given this slowdown, the IT industry is likely to undergo significant changes, including consolidation around the leading vendors and commoditization of many core technologies.

"Sounds dismal! What's a poor VC to do?"

Wait! Don't run for the windows yet! As Baron Rothschild once said, the time to buy is when the blood is running in the streets[8]. For the savvy investor, this can be an excellent time to invest. Except that the old rules

---

[8]http://www.visi.com/~contra_m/cm/reviews/cm10_rev_blood.html

don't apply. For this new environment, new strategies are needed. Here are three approaches to successful investing in this dangerous environment:

Stripping the Dead

Just as the victors of ancient battles would strip the dead of their weapons and valuables, there are assets from the carnage of the bubble that are ripe for the taking. Spinouts, PIPES, rollups, and consolidations are available across many broad segments of the tech sector. Consolidations always happen as growth industries mature. Battery's sale of the London International Financial Futures Exchange[9] to Euronext last year is a great example of profiting from consolidation. While M&A activity[10] last year was at its lowest $ level since 1994, this is due more to the cheap deals than a decline in the number of deals[11]. Buy low, sell high.

New IT Niches

Much of the carnage resulted from huge overinvestment in obvious IT niches. For many years, VCs made money on software development tools and databases, so it's not surprising to see literally hundreds of me too companies in each traditional IT market sector (VentureOne lists over 200 companies in the XML sector). But there are some signs of life in the IT wasteland. A few companies are growing at very high rates.

---

[9] http://www.liffe.com/press/releases/011029.htm
[10] http://query.nytimes.com/gst/abstract.html?res=F10F12FC3B5B0C718CDDA80894DB404482
[11] http://www.nvca.org/nvca11_18_02.html

These companies, including Battery portfolio companies Netezza,[12] Optiant,[13] and ProfitLogic[14] are markers for some significant new trends within the overall IT sector. Netezza's success is being driven by the shift from transaction processing to information extraction. Optiant is using advanced algorithms from MIT to automate business processes which leads to inventory savings of $10MM to $50MM per large company division. And Profitlogic uses proprietary algorithms to optimize prices for retailers, a vertical which has had little automation to date. Given our IT expertise, as these profitable niches emerge, we're going to be on them.

Technology Sectors Other Than IT

Even though IT and telecom represent over half of all VC spending, there have been and will be other segments. As the following chart shows, sectors like Biotech, medical devices, and semiconductors, which were ignored during the bubble have staged a dramatic comeback in the past four years, doubling or tripling their share of VC investments.

Sectors such as consumer, retailing, media, and industrial are still very small relative to their potential. Now we all know the grass is always greener in the other pasture and having the entire VC herd trample into a new pasture is a recipe for disaster (fuel cells being the latest craze!) But good VCs lead, not follow, and discover new adjacent markets that share similarities to their historical expertise.

---

[12] www.netezza.com
[13] www.optiant.com
[14] www.profitlogic.com

Consumer is a good example. In the first three quarters of 2002, consumer investments represented only 0.8 percent of VC investments. But consumer products may be the prime beneficiary of continued technical innovation. Moore's Law is still with us. Technical innovation is shifting from corporate IT to driving consumer markets. Innovation in the display industry was first driven by defense applications, then CAD, then PC, but now the action is all in the home. The Consumer Electronics Show this year was all about displays: HDTV, LCD TV's, home theater, gaming, and PDA displays are all hot. Fortunately, our portfolio company Pixelworks[15] has managed to springboard from PC displays into televisions. Communications technology is starting to hit home.

Growth in Wi-Fi is exploding and forecasted to grow to 33 million[16] units in four years. Wireless audio and video LANs will be huge. These consumer markets are big: game software at $8.3B is a bigger industry than the movie business. The worldwide market for televisions is three times bigger than that of computer displays. And consumer electronics spending is still a very small percentage of disposable income:

---

[15] www.pixelworks.com
[16] http://www.instat.com/newmk.asp?ID=388

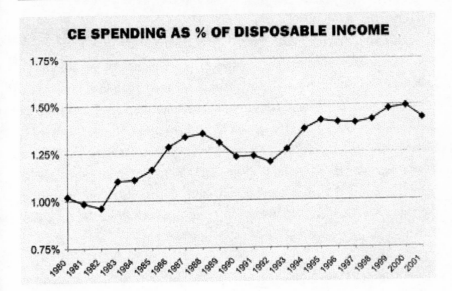

Source: SG Cowen

"Sounds plausible, but when do the LPs get their money back?"

"Show me the money!" You're going to have to wait a bit. Let's look at macro investment trends in the VC industry. The following chart shows the money invested in venture capital by year since 1980.

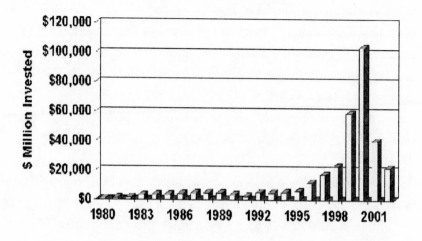

Source: VentureXpert[TM] Database by VE & NVCA

Additionally, according to VentureReporter the current investment trend is steadily down at the rate of 30 percent per year, which, if continued, would lead to 2003 and 2004 investment levels of $16 billion and $11 billion, respectively. That, together with continued cuts in fund size[17] (over $5 billion in 2002), would clean up the oversupply problem. But when do the LPs get their money?

Back to the Future

Venture Capital is a cyclical business. Like the oscillations of a spring, VC fundraising regularly rises and falls with a time constant of 3-5 years. This time constant reflects the average 3-5 year delay between an investment in a portfolio company and the return. As you would expect,

---

[17] http://www.assetnews.com/products/news/pea.html

when venture money is flush, returns for that vintage year tend to be poor, and when venture money is tight, returns for that year tend to be good. 1979 to 1985 was a boom, with the industry exploding from almost nothing to 850 firms and $3.4 billion invested in 1985. By 1991, the industry had shrunk to 450 VC firms, and only $2.5 billion invested. Yet, some of the most successful companies ever were backed during the lean years of 1985-1991, including Cisco, AOL and UUNet.

Because the Bubble was so extreme, the backlash is likely to be extreme in the other direction. Commitments to VC Funds[18] have dropped from $97 billion in 2000 to only $5.5 billion in the first three quarters of 2002, not including over $5 billion in prior commitments that VCs returned to their LPs last year. And it's only going to get worse. Joe Vicidomino of Ernst & Young estimates that of the 14,463 companies funded from 1995 to 2000, 978 went public, 1,529 were acquired, and 1,180 went out of business, leaving 10,776 companies still alive. But they're not really alive; they're zombies, walking dead. You can see them every day at VentureReporter,[19] doomed corporate souls siphoning off the dregs of the VC cash overhang, being kept barely alive until the money runs out. They still have value on VC's books, so the numbers reported by VCs[20] don't reflect the depths of the devastation. I believe it will take another 2-3 years to wash out all these zombie companies, by which time many Limited Partners will have fled the asset class. But as we have seen before, as VC gets scarce, VC returns should improve, setting us up for another boom cycle in the second half of this decade.

---

[18] http://www.nvca.com/nvca11_04_02a.html
[19] www.venturereporter.net
[20]http://www.siliconvalley.com/mld/siliconvalley/business/financial_markets/venture_capital/4773816.htm

We're at a turning point in history. This is a classic industry shakeout, and we're only half way through. The VCs who survive will be the ones who adapt to an environment of tight money and poor near-term returns. The fertile opportunities are mostly outside the traditional comfort zone of early stage IT investments. With IT markets decelerating or shrinking, money will be made in later stage industry consolidations, consumer electronics, biotech and other sectors not yet apparent. Our challenge is to evolve into adjacent sectors, without stupidly jumping into areas we know nothing about. To succeed will take hard work, intelligence, contrarianism, good investment judgment, faith, and patience. May the best venture capitalists win.

Oliver Curme has focused on investments in software and computing since he started with Battery in 1985. Some of his best investments include Aurum Software, Chordiant Software (CHRD), HNC Software, Infoseek, and Pixelworks (PXLW). Prior to joining Battery, Oliver was a lending officer in the High Technology Division of First National Bank of Boston. He holds a BS from Brown University and an MBA from Harvard Business School.

Key Strategies to Successful Venture Capital

David J. Cowan

Bessemer Venture Partners
General Partner

Evaluating Markets

Whether you're a venture investor or an entrepreneur, success depends upon your ability to identify attractive startup opportunities. To do so, professional investors most typically employ the following methodology:

(i)   Focus the fund on either high tech or life sciences, two broad sectors with strong historical returns

(ii)   Collect business plans

(iii)   Filter out those plans that don't project to yield attractive venture returns

(iv)   Carefully scrutinize the business by trying to confirm the claims made in the plan regarding market size, competition, management strength, etc.

(v)   Analyze comparable companies to confirm that private and public equity markets value this type of company with a high growth multiple

This methodology is widely proven—proven, that is, to generate weak investment returns.

When you comb through mature sectors that are ripe with proven winners, "comps" with high multiples, and dozens of well-funded competitors, you're not excelling in the craft of early stage venture capital—you're momentum investing. Momentum is critical for day traders, but it's not how you spot the next Cisco.

Furthermore, business plans are a terrible source for objective industry data. If you need the business plan to explain to you why this particular market matters, than you're in trouble, because you don't have the expertise to properly size up the opportunity. The business plan was written with the objective of attracting capital—surely you can't rely on the author to expose all the risks. (A few business plans, the best ones, do expose the major risks, but you can't rely on the author to do so.) And if the business plan sets the agenda for your research into the opportunity, then the best you can hope to do is validate what it contains, rather than come to a true understanding of how the business will fare in the marketplace.

Indeed, the marketplace is the key to identifying venture opportunities—but which marketplace? Investors typically look to the capital markets for validation—other venture investments, analyst reports, IPOs, acquisitions—when they should be spending their time researching the fundamental industrial markets in which they invest. Forget about whether investors want to buy shares of similar companies—figure out instead how many customers will pay premium prices for the company's product.

Start with the customers. Understand everything you possibly can about how the few people with big budgets (or, what's harder, lots of people with small budgets) think about their own needs and make decisions about what to buy in the face of disruptive change from technology, regulation, demographic shifts, or geopolitics (e.g. terrorism).

Usually we see the most rapid economic changes stemming from technical innovations, raising questions such as:

- When will data carriers replace their electronic data networks with optical data networks? Who makes the decision? How many units will they want? Is the price they're willing to pay consistent with high gross margins? On what dimensions will they evaluate competing solutions? And how much better than the incumbents would a startup have to be to win their business?

- How will MIS managers in mid-sized companies of 500 to 5,000 employees deal with the challenge of backing up email messages whose volumes grow 4 percent month-over-month, and how will those budget decisions get made?

- What computing tools will scientists need to comb through newly discovered genomic data in their development of new pharmaceuticals?

- How will the sales chief of a Fortune 500 company use new, wireless computers to improve the productivity of his field reps?

- What computer chips do Dell, HP and IBM need to buy for their PC products to support digital video editing?

- How can innovations in nanotechnology manufacturing be applied to medical devices?

Each of these questions centers on a different set of buyers. To properly answer them, to truly understand how buying decisions are likely to be made, an investor must specialize in one market (industry experience is not absolutely critical, but it sure helps to hit the ground running) and keep up with changes. I don't know anyone who can, with authority, answer more than one of the questions above. That's one reason why it takes a team of investors to develop a competitive, interesting portfolio of venture investments.

So the best methodology I know for identifying venture opportunities starts with a team of critically thinking investors with diversified industrial and technical experiences. Each partner investigates tectonic forces of economic change (will electric cars replace gasoline cars?; will banks outsource all their data security needs?; will indium phosphide replace silicon in tomorrow's computer chips?; how much of the U.S. call center industry will be exported to India?; and when will regulations force stock exchanges to settle trades in real time?), looking for signs that customers' budgets will shift in an important way that startups can exploit with a long-term, differentiated, defensible business. When we find these signs, we formulate an investment thesis backed up with primary data collected from buyers, as well as experts on the technology, regulatory environments, etc. All this happens before we read a single business plan.

Once we agree on a new investment thesis, we define narrow parameters around what we're looking for, sometimes down to the level of the product characteristics and management team characteristics. The theses change constantly—twice a year we meet very deliberately to refine them, but in between those meetings we actively search the industry for companies that are executing on these opportunities. Usually these are early-stage companies. Occasionally they are late-stage companies where the company already has revenue traction, and we must pay a much higher valuation in order to participate. Sometimes the company may not exist at all, in which case we will stitch together the resources from our own network of people to put such a company together. Usually we find a company comprised primarily of technical people who haven't yet sold a product and still need their first institutional round of financing.

Investment theses have a typical shelf life of two to five years before the changes have played out or, alternatively, the thesis is proven wrong. At any given time, the investors in our venture firm are typically exercising five to ten investment theses.

This process sounds like a lot of up-front work that or may or may not pay off (sometimes we can't find opportunities that align with our theses). But this approach develops our expertise in a market before we assess the business plans, which helps us avoid a lot of dumb mistakes, and makes us more helpful to our portfolio companies in our roles as board directors. It focuses us on the few markets that we think are truly the most fertile, rather than reacting to whichever business plans happen upon our fax machine. And it helps us to filter our deal flow, as we can quickly pass on business plans that don't squarely fit into one of our investment theses.

When I joined Bessemer as a technology investor in 1992, the partnership subscribed to this philosophy but didn't have a process in place for creating and maintaining road maps. I spent the first two months of my employment chasing every colorful business plan I could read (they all seemed so terrific). My bosses, the general partners of the firm, pulled me aside and suggested that I take a few months from chasing deals to develop a road map. So I spent the next three months talking to every smart person I could think of regarding information technology (Gartner analysts, Rick Sherlund at Goldman, MIS Directors, carrier technicians, successful venture investors), whittling down the known universe of thirty-eight high tech investment sectors down to four that weren't over-funded (like client server tools), over-hyped (multimedia content), outside my technical skills (semiconductor fabrication), mature (personal productivity software), too speculative (pen computing), or academic (AI). This was the best investment advice I got, and this road map exercise evolved into the firm-wide methodology described above.

Three Clues in Evaluating Entrepreneurs

When my partners and I assess company managers, we look for some key characteristics regardless of the company we're evaluating: a history of excellence, strong references from prior bosses and investors, a palpable sense of urgency, and most importantly, an open, inclusive approach by the CEO to the board of directors. Let me explain this last item.

Many if not most executives have a shortsighted approach to keeping their investors informed. They fear the personal consequences of reporting poor results—loss of credibility, responsibility, and compensation. Investors often justify this fear by responding to bad news with blame and recriminations. The result is that board members get a poor sense for the challenges in the business, and so they can't help management meet those challenges, nor can they make well-informed decisions. Consequently, when companies fail to meet their operating plans, board members grow disenchanted with the team, and have no reliable course of action other than to fire the CEO (even if the CEO's skills were not really at issue). The cycle continues.

However, my partners and I strive for a different dynamic in our portfolio companies by (i) cultivating reputations as supportive investors who respond to bad news (which is inevitable in any business) with constructive assistance; (ii) repeatedly hiring, backing and providing strong references for entrepreneurs who treat their board members as resources, not obstacles, even at the risk of their jobs; and (iii) repeatedly hiring and backing only those entrepreneurs who share our vision for candid, constructive board meetings, and who value their own reputations for putting the company first.

So when we evaluate an investment opportunity, the willingness of an entrepreneur to expose the risks and weaknesses of a plan gives us the first clue of the team's own understanding of their challenges, and their willingness to discuss them openly with investors. Even a whiff of "spin" turns us off a prospective investment, or, if we have already funded the company, compels us to immediately replace the spinner.

The second clue surfaces around questions of corporate governance. We believe that companies are best served by independent boards comprised of the CEO, two investors, and two outside directors--one with deep market experience and one with experience running a company with the same business model. Entrepreneurs who challenge this framework and try to negotiate more board control raise red flags in our minds.

The third clue is the entrepreneur's hiring pattern. Cohesion and team experience are beneficial on the engineering side, but we prefer to see a management team handcrafted from the very best candidates available, not one built around an inner circle of friends. Entrepreneurs who make all his or her friends vice presidents are either lazy or distrustful of seasoned, proven professionals. Either interpretation leads us to pass.

Our approach to active investor involvement at the board level surely isn't the only way to build successful companies (Bill Gates and Larry Ellison did just fine with almost no board direction or capital from venture investors); but it is the most reliable way, and the only way we wish to do business.

How Startup Teams Evolve

Beyond the common traits we seek out in all company managers, there are other desired characteristics that depend largely on the stage of the startup. Early stage, development companies need one set of skills, and later stage operating companies demand another (though most startups fall somewhere between the two extremes). Consequently, almost all successful management teams undergo a transition from an entrepreneurial team to an executive team.

So what do we look for in an early-stage entrepreneur? The most important factor of success is good fortune (startups are always extremely speculative), but that's obviously impossible to predict. What we do look for is a passionate, decisive risk-taker who, through personal experience as a customer or vendor, intuitively understands customer problems and purchasing behaviors in a growing market. We look for someone who can assemble scarce resources merely through the power of a vision. The successful entrepreneur paints a picture so compelling that people will quit their jobs, investors will reach into their pockets, and most importantly, customers will give them a chance. The entrepreneur must be an evangelist, a salesman, and a cheerleader.

But as a company matures, the last thing you want is a maverick taking risks at every turn. Investors who pay high, later-stage valuations demand more predictable financial performance; by the time companies go public, they are accountable for every quarter to the point where a missing penny in EPS can wipe out half their equity value.

Therefore, as companies grow they need to reduce management risk, retiring their entrepreneurial managers in favor of executives who bring deep functional experience. It takes special skills to manage the complexity of more resources, whether the resources are engineers, buildings or patents. I can't say whether it's harder to run a one-person marketing group or a 50-person marketing group, but I can say for sure that these are very different jobs.

The best entrepreneurs recognize the need for this transition, and even congratulate themselves on the day that their companies are ready to replace them with an experienced CEO.

Red Flags for Entrepreneurs

Professional investors always have a process for conducting due diligence. We walk into business plan presentations with a long list of questions that we ask every time. We do this frequently, so we are good at doing due diligence on our future business partners. But entrepreneurs raise money only once in a while, and so they just aren't as good at assessing their future business partners.

Just as we investigate entrepreneurs with due diligence, entrepreneurs ought to research their prospective venture investors. The temptation, because it is easy, is to rely on name recognition of firms and individuals as a proxy for quality and fit. That is simply naïve and lazy. What makes an investor interesting to journalists isn't necessarily the same attributes that make for an attractive business partner, such as support for companies in difficult times. Entrepreneurs can mitigate a lot of risk by cautiously checking references (both "on-list" and "off-list") – just as we do. Since all venture investors look good in the context of a "home run" investment, entrepreneurs should spend more time talking to the CEOs of companies who faced some tough challenges along the way, as most startups do on their way to success, to see how the VC differentiated himself or herself in the face of adversity.

Also, entrepreneurs should be wary of investors who do not seem to understand the entrepreneur's market. (Of course, if the investors understand the market better than the entrepreneur does, then there is another problem.) Investors who cannot even ask the tough questions should raise a big red flag because (i) they won't ask tough questions down the road, which is an important role of any good board member; (ii) they will panic about the wrong things, directing the team to spend cycles on wasteful tasks; and (iii) they are unlikely to have the right contacts to bring hires and customers. It is a bad sign if an entrepreneur has to "dumb down" his or her presentation to a venture investor. If a venture firm pressures an entrepreneur to make a decision in 24 hours or else they are going to walk, that is a bad sign. It means this firm is trying to throw its weight around and intimidate the entrepreneur rather than mutually coming to a thoughtful, beneficial decision that this partnership is good for everybody.

Entrepreneurs should think about the individual investor, not the just the firm. Whom will the venture firm nominate to the board? Will this person bring a lot of value? Consider not only the person's credentials, but whether he or she has time to put into this particular investment. There are some great venture investors who may not be attractive board members because they have too many other commitments to really spend the time that a new enterprise needs.

Risks Worth Taking

Among all the business risks—market, technology, financing, management execution, competitive, pricing, regulatory, etc. – we try to think about which ones we're willing to fund and which ones we're not. Over the years, we have grown much more comfortable funding risks that we can quantify (at least roughly) and that we can, to some extent, control. Examples are execution risk and competitive risk. Counter-examples are regulatory risk and technology risk.

I don't mean to say that we won't fund a company developing new technology. But most technologies are scientifically easy—that is they are definitely doable. But some technical projects defy the bounds of proven science – it is not obvious that anyone can actually solve the problem being tackled. So in general it would be more precise to say that we avoid scientific risk, unless (i) we believe the team to be the best team of scientists in the world to undertake this project, and (ii) there is likely no market risk in the product, such as a cure for diabetes. (Some examples in our portfolio have included American Superconductor, Ciena Communications, and ISIS Pharmaceuticals.)

The risk to which we are most sensitive is financing risk, because financing risk is the one risk that can cause you to lose more than your investment. If you invest in a company with market risk and it turns out that the market does not materialize, then you can lose our investment – and that will probably happen. If you invest in a company with financing risk where things are moving along as predicted except that it cannot finance its operations because of the financial climate, because it is poor at raising money, because a major shareholder is tapped out for future rounds, because the sector is out of favor – for whatever reason the company cannot raise enough money to finance its operations – then the investors are faced with a dilemma. You already have some cost in the business and there is a compelling argument to keep investing in the company. Not only is your initial investment at stake but your follow-on investments are at stake as well. Financing risks amplify all the other risks. The most recent crash of the technology markets underscored that lesson because the most painful losses were the ones that accumulated over several rounds of investment.

Target Multiples

The editor of this volume suggested I quantify the metrics—revenue potential, revenue growth, earnings potential, earnings growth—that we deem minimally attractive in an investment opportunity. Unfortunately, I do not think that these are the right metrics by which to establish investment hurdles. Investment hurdles should revolve around expected exit multiples on the investment, regardless of the financial metrics.

This claim seems to conflict with the principle I have repeated, probably too many times, that good venture capitalists ignore the financial markets and focus instead on the fundamentals. However, there is no conflict. The hard part of assessing investments is to understand the fundamental markets well enough to model the business's future earnings streams; the easier part is to predict how financial markets, based on ten-year trends, will value those earning streams. But both analyses are necessary.

If we were to develop a milestone based simply on expected revenue growth, we would invest only in retailers who are most likely to grow revenues into the hundreds of millions of dollars within five years. However, their breakeven is high, their margins are slim, and they have low barriers to competitive entry, and an immense capital base that is very inflexible in the face of changing consumer taste. Hence, a retailer with high revenue growth and earnings growth will still command a very low multiple on earnings.

If we were to focus simply on revenue potential, we would fund new utilities and gas-oil exploration companies. Of course, those companies face all sorts of scientific, regulatory, and technology risks that we eschew.

If we were to focus simply on gross margins, we would invest solely in software companies, which typically enjoy gross margins above 90 percent. If the companies are well run, they can reach break even quickly and show strong earnings growth as well. However, competition is very high and technology changes frequently, and so it is very difficult for a software company to sustain leadership for very long, often restricting revenue potential.

So without prejudice for minimal financial metrics, we build models based on our understanding of the fundamental business. We then apply prevailing ten year multiples of comparable companies to our models to project likely exit multiples. We typically require the model to suggest a five- to ten-times return on our investment. Generally, it is ten times for an investment where there are more risks surrounding the team and the technology. It is five times for investments that have much less risk because you already have a team and you already have some revenue.

The Role of the VC Director

Rookie entrepreneurs fear board control; experienced ones are more wary of board apathy. As a board member, I strive to be an active director who communicates with the CEO at least three times a week. I want to be consulted on every senior hiring decision. I want to be the first person the CEO calls when there is issue of relevance to the board.

One critical role of a director is to exact discipline on company management and to track them to their plan. For public companies this is not a problem because analysts do this. Everyone knows what the expectations are for a company when it announces its quarterly results. But for private companies it is very easy for the company goals to get squishy, to change with the seasons. It is easy for the company to forget about the initiative they undertook six months ago and pursued only until something "important" came up. Most importantly, it is easy for companies to simply make excuses for failing to make financial expectations without fully scrutinizing the underlying cause of the shortfall.

We view it as part of our job to show up dutifully at every board meeting and say, "Here is what you agreed last December that we could accomplish. How have we actually done?" Not to go nonlinear when the company fails to meet its objectives – no company meets all of its objectives – but to make sure the company knows that when there are variances against the plan, they are going to have to apply some thought as to why those variances are there. Once we show up a few times and ask these questions, the management team understands that this is something they have to do going into every board meeting. Of course, accountability in the boardroom is only an intermediate goal. The ultimate purpose of diligently tracking progress is to cultivate a sense of thoughtfulness about long-term strategy into daily decisions at the company.

Summary

This is the part where I repeat the most important insights into partnering with venture investors...

- Start a company because you are passionate about transforming a large market you intuitively understand. Pay no attention to the NASDAQ and IPO markets – by the time these matter to you, they will change as surely as the weather.

- Be wary of investors who don't understand your market (no matter how rich or famous they are). Rather, try to find specialists who already know, before your first meeting with them, that they wish to fund a company just like yours. These investors will be most useful to you. (Besides, if they don't fund your company, they're likely to fund your competitor.)

- Make sure that your prospective investor has capital resources for repeat investments, and time in his or her schedule to deeply engage. Conduct your own due diligence to assess patience and constructiveness.

- Force yourself to be completely up-front about the challenges of your business, from the very first pitch to the most difficult board meeting. The best entrepreneurs marry passion with intellectual honesty. Open discussions early on show off your intellect, and assure that your venture investors will be your partners, not your adversaries, down the road.

- When the day comes to hand over the reins to a new CEO, it should be a mark of your success, not failure. The best entrepreneurs usually don't stay with one company forever— rather, they have a following of investors who fund their ventures again and again.

Since joining Bessemer Venture Partners in 1992, David Cowan has made 43 early-stage investments, including 17 that have gone public, and 15 that have been acquired by public companies. David initially focused on communications technology companies such as Ciena, P-Com, and PSI-Net, and later funded network services companies such as Flycast, Hotjobs, Telocity, and Tumbleweed. In 1995 David co-founded Verisign as a Bessemer-funded spinout of RSA, serving as VeriSign's initial Chairman and CFO, and continuing today as a member of the board. He also serves on the boards of Counterpane, Finjan, Keynote, Netli, Nominum and Trigo. Previously, David worked at Oracle Corporation. He received both his M.B.A and his A.B. in computer science and math from Harvard University.

The Making of a Successful Venture Capitalist

Jonathan Goldstein

TA Associates
Partner

Profiling the Successful Venture Capitalist

Successful venture capitalists come from a wide variety of different backgrounds. There are many successful venture capitalists who were once entrepreneurs themselves. There are also successful venture capitalists who were once either lawyers or bankers. We have a couple of categories of "double Es": venture capitalists with degrees in either Electrical Engineering or alternatively English and Economics. Both have the same potential for success in the venture capital industry. In general, regardless the degree or prior profession, most successful venture capitalists tend to have a solid understanding of both technology and business strategy.

Perhaps even more important than someone's technical or educational background is his or her character. A successful venture capitalist, like any successful person, will be ambitious and driven to succeed, and will likely have a demonstrated track record of success in whatever he or she has undertaken. A successful venture capitalist will also be considered a valuable business partner by clients, and, quite simply, likable. There is a great deal of competition in the VC business and, at the end of the day, entrepreneurs will choose a venture capitalist because of the work they have done, the contributions they can make to their company's future success, and simply whether or not they like working with that person.

In my opinion, the successful VC invests in both the people and the business. Some VCs believe that if you start with the right people, they will guide you to the right business. Others believe that it is easier to change management than to change the business you are in. I think it's a risk and a pain to change either; therefore, I want to be comfortable with both before getting involved.

All that being said, however, the number-one factor in being a successful venture capitalist is to have the opportunity to invest in a bull market. But you have to remember that things are never as good as you think they are, and they are never as bad as you think they are. Like many industries, the venture business is cyclical. We had an incredible high point in the late 1990s and are trending to (what we hope is) a low point now in early 2003. We were not brilliant then and we are not stupid now. The key is to invest in great businesses and do that at reasonable prices. If you do that, you will be around in the long run.

Investment Specialization

Because we invest in later-stage companies, we are not trying to predict the future based on something that doesn't exist yet. We try to predict the future based on what exists right now. We can generally do that by consulting with industry experts when needed. So our knowledge is more byte-level than bit-level. But we are teaming up with the companies that have already shown mastery at the bit-level. We practice profitable-company investing. Many would call that later-stage investing, but we think there are plenty of later-stage companies that are unprofitable. So we stick with the term "profitable-company investing."

We think we can be most helpful to a company when they are a year or two away from a planned public offering. The companies we invest in were already successful long before we got there, so we aren't guiding them on product development. Rather, we are very involved with the strategic direction the company is taking, and helping to guide it to be most appealing to the public. In our most recent fund, our average holding period was 6.25 years. Some were much shorter and some much longer. It just depends on where the company is going and how fast it can get there.

Some funding strategies try to create brand through advertising. To me, that is a risky funding strategy: If your advertising does not work, you are out the money and have nothing to show for it. Then there are funding strategies where you end up with an underlying asset, which could potentially be useful to someone someday. Therefore, your company may not ultimately survive, but you can cover some of your investment value because you have created an asset that someone will care about. This can result in us having a decent investment even if the company may not have been a success. We have had some investments that were not successful on an operating or competitive capacity and that were sold more or less at cost, and then the other company tripled in value and our investment turned out to be pretty good.

We are active board members. Usually others look to us for guidance on issues of financing, growth, hiring, and strategy. Our involvement tends to be modulated by the management team. If the company is going public, we may be on the phone five times a week; at other times it can be quarterly board meetings with an occasional interim update call.

Motivation is probably the most important thing we try to help companies with. The reason it is important is because we own shares in the company. Fundamentally, what motivates us is to see the value of all the shares as high as possible. We are not the ones with our hands on the steering wheel and foot on the gas pedal – that is the job of the management team. To be a good director, you need to help set the company's strategy, help with the IPO process, help with positioning, and become familiar with legal and options issues. Part of it is making people feel that they are part of something bigger and giving people credit where they deserve it. I think it is always a mistake, as someone in the venture capital industry, to take credit for anything. One of my most important learning experiences came from Tom Hixon, the CEO I backed at Gulf South Medical Supply. He was always the last to take credit for something and the first to give credit to someone else. This is a great way to motivate people. You obviously have the financial methods to motivate people, but you have to make them feel like valued contributors, because they are valued contributors. And, frankly, you have to go the other way as well. If they are not valued contributors you have to replace them. These are not companies that can afford to "wait and see" with people who are not getting it done.

I like working with great entrepreneurs and great businesses. We don't confuse ourselves with being the people who made them great – they were great before we got there. Still, it is nice to be associated with companies that are successful and become industry leaders over time. In many cases, we know our experience will help these companies avoid mistakes that we and others have made in the past.

Valuation

Valuation has always been an art more than a science, although it was probably as scientific as it ever got in the early 1990s. At that point, you could look at a company that was growing at 20 percent, look at the EBITDA, multiply it by five, six, seven, or eight, and then subtract the debt – that was what the equity was worth. By the late 1990s, you could read the public company analyst reports and find five different ways to try to justify the values of some of those Internet companies. One of the things that drives us in our valuation analysis today is determining fundamentally if a company is a property that others will want to own. If this is the case, then we can pay a higher valuation ourselves. Despite the fact that we invest in growing companies and get some return by paying down debt, we are generally buying in at one entry multiple and hoping to sell at a higher exit multiple, and if the company is growing in between, we are going to get good returns. There have been times when the entry and exit multiples have been inverted, which is not a good time to invest a lot of money. And because there is a time delay, you never know.

In the case of Direct Hit, we paid an enormously high price by any historical measures; we were in at about a $125 million post-money valuation. At the time, this was a company with a couple of million dollars' worth of revenue. But when we made the investment, Ask Jeeves was trading at about $900 million in market valuation and we though Direct Hit was well positioned compared to Ask Jeeves in the consumer search business. Inktomi, which was providing OEM search services to other sites to run their searches – which Direct Hit was also doing –, was valued at the time at about $4 billion. So although $125 million was off the scale on any historical basis, we were comfortable because Inktomi and Ask Jeeves were comparable public investments we could use both in the case of an IPO and if we ended up being acquired. Ultimately Ask Jeeves ended up acquiring Direct Hit.

However, when you don't have something comparable, then entrepreneurs don't have anything they can hang their hat on. If you could look back at the business plans of some of these very successful companies and see what their true goals and aspirations were, you would see that they never projected that their companies would be worth as much as they were in 1999. And they certainly never predicted that they would be worth so much as quickly as they were in the late 1990s, in general.

High valuations have affected the pre-money valuation of companies. In the 1970s, people with "just an idea" used to get around $1 million pre-money valuation. When an investor put in $1 million, he or she would own half of the company on a post-money valuation. By the late 1990s, people with an idea had a pre-money valuation of $10 million dollars; people with an idea, an operating history, some employees and revenues, and a classic Series A could get a valuation in the teens. A Series B, or second round, could be in the $20 to $30 million range, and a Series C could be in the $60 million range. If there is a Series D, it could reach the low hundreds of millions of dollars. If you're public, it's in the hundreds, and then it trades up to the billions. I think we've seen huge inflation in companies where there is a comparable company that has already gone public because they are just trying to move the private pricing up to the public level.

We've always tried to argue that our role is one of the value-added investor who does the heavy lifting and provides the essential references. One of the things we try to make entrepreneurs realize is that if they are selling only a small portion of the company, the valuation we pay for that small part is insignificant relative to the value that we can add for the larger portion of the company.

Knowing How Much Funding to Look For

Let's say that someone is thinking about selling 33 percent of their company for $10 million, which would mean a pre-money value of $20 million and a post of $30 million. Most think that if they sold $20 million, they would be selling 50 percent of their company, but I am not sure that math applies in this space. I am not sure that investors are as rigorous when they raise the amount because they still need to have a motivated team, and the price per share will actually go up the more you raise. Investors realize you must have enough equity left over to have a motivated team.

It is always in our interest for a company to raise more money. We are going to do all the heavy lifting anyway, and I would rather do it for a $40 million investment than a $20 million investment. The issue for the company is one of valuation. Someone does not want to be diluted because of the extra portion of the company that is issued at that point in time. So if you raised all the capital the company would ever need, you would end up owning a much smaller percentage than if you had waited to do another round later on. But there's an unusual phenomenon in the Internet space that does not exist in the traditional space, and that is the value attributed to market-share leadership. Let's take the valuation methodology as price-to-revenues or price-to-customer accounts or whatever methodology you want to use to compare it to other companies. The company may be twice as big but have six times the market valuation because the multiple is three times bigger. The multiple is three times bigger because there are unusual aspects to the Internet valuations where the "firstest with the mostest" applies.

Look at Slashdot, for example, where the users are generating the content – those users aren't going anywhere else because it just keeps getting better for them. If there was someone else relative to Slashdot that had a tenth of the users they would have a thirtieth of the market value. So that argues to a company that you don't do a $2 million first round; you do a $10 million round because it is a big enough space to invest the capital and be perceived as a market leader. The reason is that getting ahead and being perceived as being ahead feeds on itself. And yes, it could be that, mathematically, the most efficient thing in terms of the percentage of the company you hold onto is to raise the amount of money instantaneously as you need it, in ever-smaller slices as you go on. But if you are trying to maximize the value of the portion of the company you hold onto, you really want to be the "firstest with the mostest" and raise a lot of money up front. In addition, you are more likely to get corporate partnerships that way, you are more likely to have to not worry about raising money again in six months, and you will have the effect of being perceived as ahead of all your competitors. You will find that that is a better strategy for maximizing the value of what you own, even if you only end up owning a fraction of what you would have the other way.

Investment Evaluation

Since we are investing in companies that don't need money, the first part of our process is to market ourselves to great companies. We contact them, visit them, and show them how we can help them. We help in several ways, including providing for shareholder liquidity needs, hopefully helping make the portion that is not sold to us worth a lot more and providing good general business advice gained from 35 years of experience with growing companies.

When we get to the point of evaluating a business, we start from the fact that it is already a good business. Our job is to figure out whether the success will continue, whether the entry price we are paying is fair, and whether someone else would likely pay more for the business several years down the line. We do this by making reference calls, and the data we collect in these calls is often very helpful to the company once we are investors.

Some extreme red flags would be entrepreneurs with a history of fraud or business dealings that repeatedly have gone bad or overly lavish headquarters. Entrepreneurs who can't explain the factors contributing to the size or growth of their market and managers who don't live within commuting distance from their company are also representatives of situations where we might opt not to get involved.

We also have to assess the risks, of course. There are a few major risks in the VC business: technology risk, financing risk, and multiple risk. Generally, you don't want to mix a risky business with a risky financing structure. You can take more business risk if you have a financing with no debt. You can take on more leverage if you have a business with very stable cash flows.

In today's environment, the biggest risk that the early-stage VCs take on is the risk that follow-on financings will be accomplished at attractive prices. The later-stage VCs take on the risk of multiple expansion/compression. That is, one risk that one has to pay a high multiple of earnings to buy into a company and that high multiple may not be available when it is time to sell. You have to really grow earnings fast to be able to handle multiple contraction and still have adequate returns.

In general, VCs try to demand high returns from their investments to compensate for the high degree of business risk (technology obsolescence, market development risk, and so on) and the illiquidity involved with private investing. In general, taking risk is a good thing if you are adequately compensated through investment returns.

Challenges

James Bond never enters a room without figuring out how he is going to get out. This process applies to the VC business as well. You must always keep in mind who will buy your stock when you are selling. In terms of timing, usually when the management team wants out, it is time to go. We tend not to control the decision, as we are typically minority investors.

Convincing companies that don't need money to take ours is another challenge. We kiss a lot of frogs, and every so often one turns into a prince. We visit thousands of companies a year just to invest in a handful. Perhaps a handful more will take our money several years later.

From the perspective of a particular company, I think everyone's challenge is hiring and retaining personnel. I think hiring good people and retaining them and motivating them is something that everyone is dealing with. Every hot company may have its moment of fame, but at some point, when it's public, people will no longer have the opportunity to get in before they IPO and get the pick-up. There is an incredibly successful company in our area called Sycamore Networks, and it is a phenomenal success story. The company went public and is now suddenly valued at $30 billion. That is tremendous. But I can't help but wonder, "How do you attract employees when the opportunity for appreciation may have largely occurred already?" It is such a great name and story, and it is run by such a great person that they may still be able to hire, but I am sure it is a challenge. Perhaps the talent will seek out the next startup and try to get in before the price runs up.

Stretching out vesting helps in holding onto people you have hired before public offerings. There is a problem, though – a problem you'd love to have, but a problem nonetheless – when a stock runs up out of control. Unfortunately, people don't really understand the underlying value of stock options. I am stunned, and I recommend to all of my companies that they can't fight the fact that all that people think about is the number of options they have, not the percentage ownership of the overall company and what the company as a whole is worth. People don't want to hear about the value, just the number they own. They want 10,000 options. They don't care about the percentage. It is an indictment of the mathematics programs in our schools, but I guess the lottery is already evidence of that. However, I am tired of trying to explain it. So now we just split the shares 10-to-1 and give somebody 10,000 shares. I have told myself for years that I don't want to hire anybody who doesn't recognize the difference, but the economy is so hot that we have run out of those people. It has actually become a marketing issue for these companies in order to have more shares to issue.

I also see the hiring crunch affecting conventional businesses that are losing employees rapidly to the Internet space. And, in the short-term, they are having a very difficult time competing. Headhunters used to do anything to capture the attention of venture capitalists because we were often a source of business for them. Now they are at a point where they don't return calls for days because they are too busy. You even see venture firms hiring headhunters internally. We are now getting very involved in the recruiting space for our companies. For example, with Direct Hit in 1999, I interviewed – or, more realistically, marketed to – all of the VP-level people who came in after our investment. In the case of Andover, things happened so quickly that the company filed its S-1 before it even had a CFO. The other thing that helps is that when you bring on a big-time venture capital firm it indicates to employees and potential hires that the company is really going somewhere. That sponsorship makes it easier to hire.

The Internet and Technology

What we have seen in the industry with regard to the Internet and the technological revolution is tension within the individual firms. The perfect example is something that happened on the West Coast: Two very well respected firms split off into separate Internet and healthcare components because they couldn't agree on where the firm should spend its time and dollars.

In our firm, we have been lucky, perhaps, that people have kept their egos in check. Even though we made a couple of investments in companies that have gone exceptionally well, we can all still see the benefit of being a part of a larger family. And basically all of us feel we are better off to be part of a diversified firm.

The difference between business-to-business and business-to-consumer is overblown. I see it as the headline without the story. A lot of people at the moment hate business-to-consumer. But just because there are some reasons to hate companies in the business-to-consumer space does not mean that you should hate all of those types of companies. The real issue with business-to-consumer and business-to-business is a comparison between the cost of customer acquisition and the lifetime value of that customer. The classic business-to-consumer company is a retailer, and it has to get on television because it is one of the best mediums by which to reach a large number of customers. But television advertising is very expensive per customer acquired, and the lifetime value of the customer in terms of the contribution margin generated is still not that much, because the business is still a retailer. The customer may buy a product now but not come back to your site for ten years. For example, Furniture.com is getting a lot of excitement, but how often do people buy sofas and what is the lifetime value of their customer? Drugstore.com may be a better model, because people need to buy prescriptions and drugstore items every month or so. Their lifetime value as a customer is better because they may be spending more on a recurring basis. However, I don't use more shaving cream just because I am a Drugstore.com customer. It is incredibly convenient and I have moved some market share to them, but I do not use more of the underlying product.

Now let me contrast that to Datek. I used to trade maybe ten times a year. Now I have Datek on my screen at all times with their streamer flashing at me to alert me to situations where I might want to make more trades. And so the number of trades I make in a year has now gone up significantly. So when you look at business-to-consumer, the real issue is looking at the cost to acquire customers and the lifetime value of the contribution margin of that customer.

Many business-to-consumer concepts fail there – it costs too much to get a customer and the real value of the customer is not there, and ultimately they will run out of capital. Contrast that with business-to-business: You might have a much narrower group of customers, and therefore you know that you have to go after these 500 in a very targeted way, so it doesn't cost as much to actually acquire the customers. Then the lifetime value of a customer from a contribution margin standpoint is also much higher, because in the business-to-business space people are typically reordering monthly. I think many people talk about business-to-business and business-to-consumer but do not take it to that next level of analysis.

There will be people on the business-to-consumer side who take it to that next level and will be incredibly successful. However, if you put 1,000 business-to-business companies next to 1,000 business-to-consumer companies, will they do better on average? In my opinion, yes.

The keys to building a successful Internet company include attracting key employees, motivating key employees, coming up with smart financing strategies, taking advantage of what is given to you, being able to be nimble and adjust strategies when necessary, knowing how to handle and deal with competitive threats, and being able to deal with moral and ethical issues, to name just a few. It is no different than other non-Internet businesses, but in this industry, in general, you have individuals who are young and inexperienced. That does not mean that they cannot be great executives; it just takes some time.

Jonathan Goldstein focuses on Healthcare, technology, and service-related businesses investment opportunities for TA Associates. Prior to joining TA Associates in 1986, Jonathan worked in the Protein Chemistry and Cell Biology Departments of Biogen, Inc. He has been published on the subject of the scale-up of recombinant animal cells, and holds a U.S. patent. He serves on the Board of numerous leading Internet and healthcare related companies.

Jonathan has sat on several Boards including, at present, J&B Software, Inc., New West Management Services, Inc., NuGenesis Technologies Corporation, and WellMed Medical Management, Inc. And formerly, on Andover.Net, Inc., Direct Hit Technologies, Inc., Gulf South Medical Supply, Inc., Preferred Payment Systems, Inc., and Unique Instruments, Inc.

Jonathan holds an SB in Biology from Massachusetts Institute of Technology (1983), an SB in Chemical Engineering from Massachusetts Institute of Technology (1984) and an SM in Biomedical Engineering from Massachusetts Institute of Technology (1986). Additionally, Jonathan holds an MBA from Harvard Business School (1990).

Jonathan's other professional affiliations include serving on the Board of Associates Executive Committee for the Whitehead Institute for Biomedical Research, sitting on Boston's Museum of Science Investment Committee, serving as the MIT Class of 1983 Secretary and Reunion Co-Chairman, and serving on the Board of the New England Venture Capital Association.

Venture Capital – Beginning to End

Praveen Gupta

CDIB Ventures
Partner

Finding the Right VC Firm

The road to success for entrepreneurs requires companions who have the experience and are willing to support and navigate them through the journey. Venture Capitalists are probably the strongest companion entrepreneurs would need to achieve their goals. This makes it very critical for the entrepreneur to find the right companion for their journey. They need to think of this as a dating game leading to a successful marriage. Task of finding the right venture capital firm should be treated as a full-time job at least for the first-time funding.

The best connection between an entrepreneur and a venture capital firm is a mutual acquaintance. Venture capitalists put a lot of weight to investment opportunities coming through people they know and trust. VCs network heavily and seek opportunities through this network as well as leverage this network to add value to their investee companies. It is best to get an introduction to a VC through someone that both the entrepreneur and the VC know and respect. Once the introduction is made, the VCs often lend a more favorable ear to the entrepreneur and are more willing to spend time with them. There is a very high probability that the VCs will not respond to unsolicited executive summary or a cold call. The VCs usually have very tight schedules juggling multiple tasks at hand. They get hundreds of calls and business plans a month. They physically do not have time to attend to every business plan and cold call. The best way for entrepreneurs to connect with a VC is to network as much as they can, talk to other startup companies, professional firms, and successful entrepreneurs to find their way into the venture capital firm.

The entrepreneurs need to truly research venture capital firms who invest in their space. It is easy to get a list of all VCs from the web. There are several directories available such as National Venture Capital Association's directory. The entrepreneur should match their proposed venture with the focus and criteria of the VC under consideration. They must look at their portfolio and avoid the VCs with investment in competing companies. Geography is also a factor to consider. They should evaluate the added value expected from the VCs and match it with the value that the VCs can add to their venture at the current stage of their Company. It is always best to get smart money than passive money. Highly experienced VCs have gone through the startup process over and over again and can navigate the entrepreneurs through pit falls in their journey. They can bring their vast network to help the company succeed.

It is very critical for an entrepreneur to learn as much as possible about the VC they expect to meet before their initial presentation. The entrepreneur should really research the background of not only the firm, but also the partner they are meeting with. They should think about the VC as a business partner and not just an investor. The entrepreneurs should try to ask all the questions they can to build up a mutual trust and respect. The questions should focus on things such as: How does the business fit into the VC's general investment focus? What kind of value will they add as an investment partner? How will they add that value? Entrepreneurs should ask for information that will help them do their due diligence on the VC, just like VCs perform due diligence on the Company. Entrepreneurs should not be afraid to ask these questions. There is always a possibility that the VC already has a conflicting investment, so they might listen and get some information but not pay much attention. Most VCs will tell the entrepreneurs up front if they have a conflicting investment in their portfolio and avoid a waste of critical time for both sides. The entrepreneur needs to know if the VC is really active in the area in which the company is trying to launch its product. If the VC is not active in that space, then the efforts to get VCs attention will be a waste of time. Before making the presentation, the entrepreneur should be sure to have done the background work on the venture capital firms. They will know what the VC is looking for and what the VC's knowledge level may be.

Entrepreneurs tend to get emotional about their ideas and plans. However, VCs are looking for passion and an open mind. This is important since the VCs tend to play devil's advocate during the presentation. As this may be a bit unnerving for the entrepreneurs, they should be very careful and objective about what they say and how they present. The presentation should be a well-balanced overview of the business plan. It should clearly show the vision, depth of knowledge and understanding of the technology, target markets, customers, and their roadmap for success. It is up to the Entrepreneurs to convince the VCs by satisfactorily supporting their cause through facts and logic behind their beliefs. They should not be focused on one or two areas such as product, technology, markets, or the team. The bottom line is that many VCs make up their initial decision in the first few minutes of the presentation. The rest of the time they are either really interested or they are just sitting there out of courtesy. In the initial meeting, it is important to be gentle and just gauge the match. On the entrepreneur's side, they should watch out for VCs who are gathering lots of information but not taking any action. They need to make sure that the VCs are not just collecting information and passing it on to someone else. That is why checking the background of the VC is critical. Most VCs are very ethical and will not engage in such activities. They want to do the right thing, but then there are always exceptions in the real world. The entrepreneurs need to be sure to do the background check and speak with peers in the industry.

Evaluating a Potential Investment

Venture capital firms review hundreds to thousands of ideas annually. They also network with their peers, industry experts, and potential customers in a given industry, and stay aware of voids that exist in their target industry. Typically the venture capital firms stay up to speed on their target industry through professional material available in magazines, seminars, trade shows, the Web, etc. They will also network very closely with industry experts, customers, and related professionals. If a new Company comes along and the VC is not already familiar with their type of products, they will research the literature, explore their network, and determine the value proposition of the new product. This is a fairly methodical and quick process. VCs will also quite often learn from their portfolio companies. Regardless, the initial onus of locking in VCs' interest lies on the entrepreneurs' shoulders.

As the VCs come across entrepreneurs with great ideas, they are trying to match the voids with the ideas to determine the potential opportunities for investment. Sometimes, the idea may not be obvious but may be teasing enough for the VCs to investigate the space further and determine if the idea solves a real problem and if there are any practical solutions available. All this legwork, before and after the idea becomes known, leads the VCs to the right opportunity in their minds for their investment. Sometimes, the VCs may themselves seek entrepreneurs to take an idea to fruition into the market based on their own knowledge and understanding of the industry.

A successful idea has clarity, vision, uniqueness, and feasibility. It solves a real problem. The entrepreneur must be able to show their vision to the venture capitalists very quickly in their initial presentation. The key items that VCs are looking for include:

- Is the solution addressing a real problem and fulfilling a customer need?
- Is it practical and realistic?
- Does the team know and understand their customers?
- Is the team experienced and knowledgeable?
- Is there real market for the product? If yes, how large and its status?
- Is the technology real and feasible?
- Do true and high barriers to entry exist?
- What is the competitive landscape?
- Is the business model and financial plan realistic?
- Can we play a role in the Company's success?

If the entrepreneur cannot answer above questions satisfactorily at the initial meeting then most likely the VC will not move forward to the next step. The VCs expect logical and convincing answers to the above questions. It is easy for VCs to differentiate hype with reality as they have gone through many cycles of developing a startup company into a successful venture.

If the VCs are interested in the company, they then evaluate the overall business model. They have a general understanding of the investment space that is being targeted; they know the type of business models that will work in a particular space. The VCs are really looking for a realistic venture. It should bring real benefit to the customers. It should either address a large existing market through a significantly better and more efficient solution or create a very fast and high growth new market in the industry space. VCs will evaluate the assumptions underlying a business model very closely and determine whether they are practical and realistic. Do they match the well-known practices in the industry? Are there barriers to success of the model that cannot realistically be addressed? Answers to these questions give VCs a clear picture of whether the business model is worth pursuing.

Venture capital firms are not interested in models that are too optimistic and do not address the potential issues that might come up, the roadblocks that might emerge, and so on. For example, most entrepreneurs come from technical backgrounds and they tend to be highly optimistic. They think they can develop a product in a very short type frame, and accordingly their budget estimation is low. But when reality sets in and they really start executing, it takes much longer and larger amount of funds to achieve their goals. Having worked with several startups, VCs have a feel for what will it take for the company to develop a successful product and launch it to sell to their customers. In analyzing a business model, VCs are looking to see if the company's projections fall within the general statistics for what it takes for a company to succeed in their industry space. VCs also look to see if the company is truly addressing the market that the product is designed for.

In valuing a company, key items to look for are the management team, technology, market opportunity, growth rate, customers, and potential for a liquidity event. The overall value of a company is based on a combination of these items and their current status – is it just a concept or does the company have a product that is already selling? Other important factors are things such as investor pool – who are the current investors in the company, and are they willing to stand up and help the company any further? What kind of intellectual property does the Company have? Are there any significant patents awarded to the Company?

Valuation of a Company depends on its stage of development. Earlier stage valuation is based on a combination of monies being raised, desired ownership by the investor syndicate for the investment amount, and typical prevailing valuations for the stage. Later stage valuation may tie into the discounted multiples based on public markets at the time of investment and possible multiples at the time of a potential exit event. The VCs will perform their own math to determine their potential return and match it with their desired return to meet their fund's goals. There are some valuations statistics available in the marketplace. The entrepreneurs and the VCs could use these as benchmarks alike.

Venture capitalists value the company from a long haul perspective, keeping their potential returns in mind and discounting for their value-added personal efforts going into the company and potential failure scenarios. Their goal is to provide better than public market returns to their limited partners. Other investment professionals such as investment banking or M&A are generally valuing a company based on comparable public market multiples with short-term in mind and based on the current status with future visibility based on various quantitative information. VCs do not have such visibility since the startup companies typically are still building the products or services and have to go through uncharted waters quite often. The market could be shifting as they develop the product. Generally, venture capital firms are going in during earlier stages when companies have none to little revenues and customer traction. VCs are really going after the team – how good the team is, and then look at how viable the market is, how good the technology is, how good the patent portfolio is, etc.

In terms of a management team, the key elements are the passion, attitude, and knowledge of their markets and customers. They need to understand their customers well so they can pinpoint the exact voids that customer faces with available solutions. This requires market, technology, and competitive landscape knowledge, customer contacts, and experience of having gone through the process in their careers. The team should be open to criticism, ready to steer through the turbulent periods, adjust to the market and customer needs. They should be team players not individuals. An extensive relevant Rolodex is an extremely valuable asset. Beyond that, VCs look at the management team's track record and background. Quite often they will perform background checks. Experience with startups or turned around situations in the past is always very helpful. If the management team has significant connections in the industry, there is a good chance they can get to where they want to go. Of course, VCs too bring a strong Rolodex to the table, but it always helps for the management team also to have their network.

Growth Potential and Risk

Growth potential in venture capital industry relates to the expectations of venture capital firms' limited partners. Certain expectations of return are set with the limited partners when the funds are raised. In general, the expectation is to beat the returns from the alternative investments such as public markets, real estate, etc., over the life of the fund. Venture capital firms are looking to achieve this goal through their investments in startup companies.

This expectation ties back to the growth potential of the company under consideration. If the company is growing at 10 to 15 percent a year and VCs think that their investment is only going to get 10 to 15 percent return, it is not interesting enough for the VCs to move forward with an investment. Venture capital firms will typically look for a hockey stick type of ramp up in sales and profits once the product is shipping with concrete data to back up their claims. Obviously, there is lots of guesswork in projections at early stages of a company. VC's confidence level in the team's execution ability to get to this stage is also a major factor. The time to market is critical and adds to the risk of investment. To hedge such risks, VCs will typically look for CAGR in high double to low triple digits. They will validate the growth through their professional network and their own knowledge of the space.

Setbacks in venture capital investments are bound to happen. There may be few home runs, some average returns, and few failures among the investments of a venture capital fund. To average this out, the VCs will look at the potential exit valuations of the investee companies and their possible ownership in them combined with the funds invested. An evaluation of this equation effectively provides the potential return on investment. This needs to be significantly higher than overall target return for the fund since there is too much subjective analysis involved.

In evaluating potential ROI, venture capital firms look at their ownership in the company, the state of public markets, liquidity event time frame, and the Company's potential market cap at the time of a liquidity event. Simple math provides a rough idea of potential return based on ownership and potential market cap at the time of liquidity event. Venture capital firms then look at their criteria for the overall fund and account for the setbacks. VCs attempt to achieve much higher than 25 percent IRR for their fund over its life, which is typically seven to ten years.

VC business is a high-risk business and risk taking is part of the game. The basic question is what level of risk are VCs willing to take? VCs look at it in different ways. Those who are willing to take higher risk for higher reward go for earlier-stage companies, and those who are looking for lower risk go for later-stage companies. VCs know that there will be failures. These failures must be hedged. Experienced VCs can spot problems ahead of time and seek proactive actions to hedge the risk. There are no right or wrong answers to any problems. VCs will determine all pros and cons based on known information and decide on whether the risk is worth pursuing. Obviously, there need to be lot more pros than cons for the risk to be worth it. Once the cons are understood and appear to be controllable, the VCs will be willing to move forward and work towards mitigating the risks and watch for potential risks.

Points of Caution

The worst mistake entrepreneurs can make is to get too emotional and maintain a tunnel vision. When this happens, entrepreneurs start thinking as individuals rather than as a team. When starting a company they need to be open to criticism – not only from investors but also from their team members including the most junior employee in the company and even family and friends. They need to be willing to listen to why someone is making a particular critique and then work on it and see what they can do to make the situation better. It may be that the entrepreneur is right, but they should still be listening. Good entrepreneurs are not ruled by emotion – they keep their passion and are open to criticism. The entrepreneurs should provide motivating leadership to their team regardless of their title and avoid selfish attitude. The key to success for the entrepreneurs and their team is to stay focused, be realistic, admit mistakes, fix them, learn from them, and move on.

Attitude of entrepreneurs during the due diligence and term sheet negotiation phase could raise significant red flags for the venture capital firms. When VCs are considering investment, they really want to learn everything about the company. They want to learn about the background of the entrepreneur and the team, about the source of technology, etc. Due diligence phase can unveil inconsistencies in the claims by the company and the reality within the company. Any attempts to hide the information or hesitation in providing information are potential red flags. The inconsistencies in the market data are not a major issue for the VCs, but inconsistencies in presenting facts about the company, technology, people, and their background, can be bad news. Venture capital firms cannot afford to get into a relationship with someone who is fabricating the truth on the other end. VCs generally want to come in as partners and play an active role in the company's success. Entrepreneurs should treat them as such. The due diligence phase is a courting phase building trust and respect for a future long-term partnership.

Entrepreneurs should watch out for the situation where the VCs are gathering detailed information without any feedback or action on their part. They should also look for signs where the VCs are not being open with answering questions related to their background, focus, other portfolio companies, etc. A thorough research on VCs is very important. It is best to perform due diligence on the VCs to feel comfortable.

It is quite likely that entrepreneur raises too little money. Majority of the entrepreneurs have technical backgrounds. They have tendency to underestimate the cost of taking a product from concept to launch and into profitability due to lack of their general management background. It is best for the entrepreneurs to find a mentor with a general management background or someone who has gone through a startup company building process before. Such professionals can help build a realistic business plan to evaluate the right size of funds to be raised.

It is very helpful to have multiple firms as part of the funding syndicate. As subsequent rounds of funding take place, single investor may not be able to support the Company in the long run if it becomes tough to raise funds from outside sources due to business conditions. Multiple firms can pool their resources and carry the company through tough times as long as the company is performing well. This also makes it very critical to pick the right venture capital firms who have a track record of continued support for well performing portfolio companies. It will always help to talk to venture capital firms' portfolio company management as part of entrepreneurs due diligence on the venture capital firm.

Term Sheets

A term sheet is not a commitment by the VC; it is a statement of interest in investing in the company. The terms given in the term sheet are very generic and non-binding. As the legal process starts there will be many minor issues that arise, but the entrepreneur needs to be aware of those things and look at them later as individual items. Basically the entrepreneur should be looking for not only the valuation and the investment amount that the VC is putting through the term sheet, but also what kind of added value the VC is bringing to the company. They should balance what the term sheet says with what they know about the

VC in terms of added value. Many entrepreneurs get hung up on valuation. The overall future valuation of a company could be significantly higher with proper partners even if the initial valuation is somewhat lower.

Many of the terms in the term sheet may not seem significant initially, but could have long lasting effect on the future dealings of the company. The entrepreneurs should look for whether or not the term sheet provides enough incentives for the team for them to achieve their goals. Generally, VCs will want to make the company successful. They are very sensitive to this goal. The term sheet also serves to demonstrate the attitude of the VCs to the entrepreneur. Entrepreneurs need to remember that the VCs are there primarily for investment purposes while willing to help the company become successful. They need to get a reasonable rate of return. At the same time the entrepreneurs need to remain more diligent because they have to have an investment in the company. They also need to make sure that they have a competent attorney to help them close the deal. There will be many legal items that the entrepreneurs may not be familiar with and these may have long lasting effects.

Venture capital firms typically take preferred shares for their investments. Founders, employees, and other professionals will most likely have common shares. Preferred shareholders get preferred rights in exchange of paying a higher price per share compared to the price of common shares.

Understanding some key vocabulary is crucial to reading a term sheet. There are many areas to understand, but below are a few that are highly important. Following terms and rights typically relate to preferred shares.

Dividends: Dividends are a certain percentage, typically 8 percent, to be paid to the investors on an annual basis if and when declared by the Board of Directors. In practice, the Board of Directors in a pre-IPO Company rarely declares dividends. The dividends could be cumulative or non-cumulative.

Liquidation Preference: Liquidation preference is critical in case of an M&A or company closure situation. A very high liquidation preference might not leave anything for the employees and other common shareholders in case of liquidation through an M&A or closure. The liquidation preferences may add up if you have multiple rounds before any of the above situations materialize. While looking at liquation preferences, entrepreneurs should really look at potential M&A scenarios and see how the distribution of funds would take place and how much funds would be left for the common shareholders. In case of closure, most likely there will not be much left to distribute to anyone. Usually, VCs will try to set the liquidation preferences in a way that would leave a reasonable size of funds for the common shareholders in case of a liquidity event. The liquidation preferences could be participating or non-participating for the preferred shareholders. In participating liquidation preference, the preferred shareholders first get their distribution and then share balance of the funds with the common shareholders on as-converted basis. In non-participating liquidation preference, the preferred shareholders get their distribution first followed by the common shareholders taking balance of the funds.

Conversion Rights: This provides a right to convert preferred shares to common shares at any time at the option of the shareholders. The preferred shareholders may individually exercise this right if the M&A liquidity event brings very high valuation and conversion provides higher returns compared to liquidation preference. The conversion is generally automatic in case of liquidity via an Initial Public Offering (IPO) or by election of predefined percentage of preferred shareholders.

Redemption Rights: This provides a right to redeem preferred shares after certain period at the original purchase price. The period is typically 5 to 7 years. This may happen if a liquidity event has not taken place within this period, and the investors don't see any possibility in near future at the time of expiry of the redemption period. Redemption rarely takes place for pre-IPO companies.

Anti-dilution Clause: This is only applicable if the valuation may go down in the follow-on round. This is extremely common during a downturn in the economy since the companies generally get funded at higher valuations during the high tide of the economy. Anti-dilution adjustment has an effect of issuing more shares of the prior preferred series to the existing investors to maintain their original ownership in the company for their investment in the Company. Obviously, this has a further diluting effect on the common shareholders. If this clause is enforced, new VCs might require maintaining the Employee option pool size at a reasonable percentage of the outstanding shares depending on the stage of the Company and hiring requirements resulting in further dilution for the common shareholders. In practice, expected anti-dilution adjustment never materializes to the fullest extent since new investors require the anti-dilution on a pre-money basis and the calculations end up in an infinite loop. Common shareholders do not have a right to adjustment for anti-dilution. There are always certain exclusions for anti-dilution clause to kick in. These may include additional options for the employee option pool, warrants to banks, additional shares on conversion, etc. There are two types of anti-dilution clauses.

1. *Full Ratchet Anti-dilution adjustment*: This method has an effect of adjusting the prior round share price downward for the lower valuation in the latest round.

2. *Weighted Average Anti-dilution adjustment*: This method has an effect of adjusting the prior round share price downward based on a formula using share count and prices in current and prior rounds. There are three types of weighted average adjustments. Narrow-Based weighted average takes into account all the preferred shares outstanding for the particular series to be adjusted. Middle-of-the-Road weighted average takes into account all issued and outstanding shares, i.e. excluding the convertible items such as debt, options, and warrants. Broad-Based weighted average takes into account all outstanding shares.

Voting Rights: These rights allow preferred to vote on as-converted basis similar to the common shareholders. It may be that all the preferred shareholders will vote as a single class, or maybe each class will vote separately. This applies to all matters submitted to a vote of shareholders as allowed by the law.

Protective Provision: This provision asks for certain voting rights on issues that adversely affect the shareholder rights and should be approved by the preferred shareholders in the future. For example, if the company is increasing the authorized shares, creating new class of securities senior to current class, redemption of shares, change of authorized size of the Board of Directors, change of rights, M&A, etc.

Board Composition: The lead investor will most likely request one or more Board seats on the new Board of Directors after the financing is complete. The Board size and its composition are defined in this clause. Typical Board may consist of the CEO, one common representative, one or more investors, and one or more industry experts. Board size should be maintained at a manageable size. Five is fairly common and manageable Board size.

Special Board Approved Items: The investors may require that certain items being approved by the Board must have consent of their representative on the Board. These items can include any major expenses, loans, contracts, executive staff hiring and firing, etc. Basically, the investors do not want to give a blank check to the CEO. The Entrepreneurs need to make sure that these requests are not unreasonable for running the corporation on a day-to-day basis.

Information Rights: The investors will require that certain information about the company should periodically be provided to them. The information generally includes financial statements, business status, etc. A threshold may be set to exclude smaller investors from getting the information too frequently. Generally, every investor will get the information at least on an annual basis.

Registration Rights: These relate to the IPO. There are three types of registration rights, viz., Demand, Piggyback, and Form S-3. Demand rights set the conditions for an IPO on demand by the shareholders. This will include minimum lapsed period since investment, size of offering, etc. Piggyback rights allow certain percentage of shares held by the investors to be included at the time of the IPO subject to cutback at underwriter's discretion. Typically, investors require 25 to 30 percent of their holding as part of the piggyback registration rights. Form-S3 rights allow multiple subsequent registrations of securities with certain minimum offering each time to get the liquidity after IPO. Typically investors are locked out for at least six months through a lockup provision in the term sheet. SEC Rule 144 also governs lockup period.

Right of First Offer: This allows the investors to purchase their pro-rata shares in any subsequent financing to maintain their percentage ownership in the Company.

Right of First Refusal, Co-Sale: This allows the investors a right of first refusal, subordinate to the Company's rights, and a co-sale right on the sale of shares by founders, other investors, or change in control of the Company. There could be exclusions to these rights. There is certain time period allowed for the Company and shareholders before such sales are permitted.

Transfer Rights: Transfer rights allow the shareholders to transfer their shares to others on a conditional basis. There are some exclusions – for example, founders can give a certain amount of shares to their family members or estate. Also, investors are allowed to transfer their shares to their partners or related entities.

Employee Stock Option Pool: VCs fully support incentives for employees through grant of stock options. The term sheet will specify the option pool size as well as the vesting rules. Generally, the options will vest over a four-year period at a pre-determined periodic rate. The desired size of the option pool depends on the stage of development of the Company. Typical size is 20 percent of the outstanding shares available for grant as options to the employees. Late stage companies may have much smaller employee option pool size. Company's head count growth is the major factor in determining size of the pool.

Key Person Life Insurance: The investors require a Key Person Life Insurance policy for certain reasonable amount for the team members deemed critical to the success of the company. The investors require this insurance to protect their investment to certain extent in case of death of key employees.

Invention Assignment: The investors will require that each employee and consultant should enter into a confidentiality and invention assignment agreement with the Company. This is required to insure that all of the Company intellectual property is protected and belongs to the company.

Indemnification: The investors will require that the Company indemnify all Directors and the investors of the Company to the broadest extent permitted by law. They will also require that a Director and Officer's liability insurance be maintained by the Company. This is required to protect the Directors of the Board from potential lawsuits by the shareholders, employees, or third parties.

Above definitions provide only a conceptual idea of various terms used in a term sheet. Actual legal documents, based on the term sheet, will contain many more details expanding upon these terms. Only an attorney can help the entrepreneur to understand the nitty-gritty details and pros versus cons of each item.

Roles and Strategies of the VC

The VC's role depends on the stage of the company. For a later-stage company the role is not very active, but they will still provide help in networking as well as bring partners and customers to the table. If it is an early- or middle-stage investment they will most likely take a Board seat or at least a Board Observer role and be fully involved. That role would include things such as mentoring the management team, helping define the company strategy, introducing them to potential customers, helping them recruit and fill management vacancies, and so on. The VCs certainly do not want to micromanage; rather, they keep their involvement very high-level, from a Board perspective.

Investment strategies tend to shift somewhat with the economic cycle. The ideal investment outcome is an IPO, but in a down market that might not be possible. The next best thing is M&A. What is happening today goes back to what happened in the pre-1997 timeframe. The VC industry might be trending to go to an extreme, but it will swing back a little bit. The industry will stabilize at a level similar to the pre-1997 timeframe and resume its normal growth. Investment amounts per deal have already gone to pre-1997 levels, and the investment principles have also gone back to those levels. The only issue is that in the last three to four years VCs have been burned so much that they are a little nervous about making new investments right now. In the next year or two the VCs will recover from the shock and complete the consolidation of their portfolio. The VC investment cycle will get back to its roots of 80s and early 90s

In terms of specific strategies, VCs are very careful in their due diligence. They are looking for a reason to reject the deal as opposed to a reason to do the deal. They tend to cover all the bases, don't assume things, and don't take the entrepreneurs solely on their word. Often VCs get emotional too, just like entrepreneurs. This is very true particularly in case of follow-on investments. Many of the VCs come from an investment banking or operational background, and by human nature they are emotional about things they have done in the past. The key is not to mix the emotion with the business and the investment. Have a partner attitude with a realistic approach. As a VC, one of the things they should really enforce in their portfolio company is, "We all, as a team, need to do whatever is needed to steer the Company to success." However, the VCs should not go in with the attitude, "We own a part of this company and they [company] have to do what we tell them to do."

There are three golden rules for VCs:

(1) *Know your industry before you invest*: It is hard to judge the value proposition of an entrepreneur's idea until and unless you are familiar with the space to which the idea applies. Certainly, no one can be master of everything. However, a general knowledge and significant network in the related industry is always helpful in appreciating the value proposition. Keep your antenna up all the time.

(2) *Management team is the key*: A weak team can lead an excellent idea to failure and an excellent team can make an average idea very successful. It's all about execution, experience, knowledge, and leadership. The team must be checked out very thoroughly ahead of all other elements of the company under consideration once the value proposition of the idea has been established.

(3) *Be a partner, Not an owner*: Venture capital industry is all about successful investments in innovative ideas. To increase the shareholder value, the VCs have to invest significant effort in building successful companies. Such efforts can be successful only if the VCs go in with a "partner" mindset rather than an "owner" mindset. An "owner" mindset alienates the company resulting in lack of cooperation from them. As a result there are no winners. Just like VCs expect entrepreneurs to be open-minded, so should be the VCs.

On the entrepreneur's side, there are five golden rules:

(1) *Be passionate, not emotional*: Passion for your dream is what makes you successful. Emotions will limit your vision and you will get blind sided in your road to potential success. Passion will get your creative juices flowing and show you the path to your success.

(2) *Seek a partner, not an investor*: As an entrepreneur, you need all the support you can get to achieve your dreams. A passive financial partner will provide you the money but will probably receive the biggest bang for your efforts once you succeed. You want to seek a partner who brings in "smart-money," i.e., cash along with experience and contacts in an active role.

(3) *Have a realistic vision, not simply a dream*: As an entrepreneur seeking VC funding, you need to be realistic about what you are trying to achieve. VCs are not thrilled about idea becoming reality in a hundred years. They would rather see the idea become reality in a much shorter time-span bringing them success and liquidity in a reasonable time frame within the life span of their fund. It is good to push the boundaries, but constraints should not be forgotten.

(4) *Assemble "A-Team"*: The team is number one element in achieving success. Team quality can make or break a company. The entrepreneurs should not try to hang on to the top title. They should fill the positions with the required talent and be a motivating leader in psychological sense rather than a job title.

(5) *Prove flexibility for "Future" adjustments*: The entrepreneur should always maintain an open mind. They should take criticism in a constructive manner and act on it to improve themselves and chances of success for their company.

Praveen Gupta is an experienced venture capitalist. His investment focus is early to late stage ventures developing communications infrastructure and Internet enabling technologies including Telecom Networks, Enterprise Networks, Applications Software, and Communications Semiconductors. Praveen is actively involved at the Board level in his portfolio companies and actively mentors the entrepreneurs. His prior experience includes program and engineering management of telecom/datacom and related product development and launch in multiple technology industries. He has held senior level technical and business operations management positions at Lucent, Ericsson, Fujitsu-ICL, and Halliburton. He has successfully planned and launched several communications and networking products into the global market while providing technical direction and guiding various corporate functions. Praveen has Masters Degrees in Physics (University of Roorkee, India), EE (Indian Institute of Science, India), CS (University of Texas), and an Executive M.B.A. from Golden Gate University.

Strategies, Risks and Opportunities in Venture Capital

Mathias Schilling

Bertelsmann Ventures; BV Capital
Partner; General Partner

Keys to Successful Venture Capital Relationships

A successful relationship between venture capitalists and entrepreneurs is built on mutual trust and respect. Given the ups and downs that every venture is bound to face, it is important for both parties to align interests, early in the process, by managing each other's expectations. With early stage companies, entrepreneurs should expect the venture capitalists to contribute tangible value through pragmatic guidance, strategic relationships, and mutually agreed upon sum of capital. Venture capitalists expect entrepreneurs to responsibly manage the capital investment by leading and motivating employees, executing upon an operating plan, and making the proper strategic and tactical business decisions.

The venture capital "ecosystem" is based on long-term relationships where credibility is very important. The lifeblood of every venture capital fund is its ability to attract high-quality, proprietary deals. By overwhelming margins, proprietary deals are referred to our fund by sources that are trusted and respected within the technology community. Given the number of deals that are sent to our fund, it's critical for the entrepreneur to be introduced by one of these trusted sources. A qualified recommendation assures the venture partner that the deal has not been "over-shopped" and has been screened by the trusted sources. These sources are usually familiar with our fund's target investment criterion and will qualify whether the opportunity matches. Every deal that we received is scrutinized to determine its compatibility to our investment criterion. If attractive, we will usually invite the company in to make a formal presentation.

We try to keep meetings with entrepreneurs very focused on the opportunity at hand, the competitive advantage the company possesses, and why they believe the opportunity is attractive for investment. We prefer that the company displays as little hype as possible, and instead focuses on emphasizing milestones – those already reached, as well as those on the horizon. There's a big difference between a sales presentation and a VC presentation. When I feel like I'm being oversold, the presenter loses significant credibility.

A venture capitalist's primary responsibility is to invest in high growth opportunities in a manner that provides significant opportunity for upside benefit, while managing downside risk. We do not try to structure the toughest and tightest deal but try to make sure that we align our interests with the entrepreneur early on. Typically, investors are adamant about several points: valuation (which determines the total ownership stake in an investment), protective provisions (which make sure that investors have a say in major corporate events), dilution provisions (to maintain ownership stake in future funding rounds), board structure (which helps determine ease/difficulty in getting Board initiatives passed) and liquidation preferences (which determines how much capital is distributed to investors in various classes before the common shareholder participates).

From our firm's perspective, we prefer to have a syndicate of investors participate in a funding round. The number depends on what stage the company is at. Given our fund's focus on early-stage, two investors is usually fine. The prospect of managing more investors rarely thrills entrepreneurs, however, I believe that over the long run, more investors provide precious expertise, experience, and relationships.

A Company's Value

In the evaluation process we consider many variables (management, technology, market, differentiation, financial aspects) to determine the value of the company. We look to invest in markets that are potentially large and growing fast. We try to avoid "me too" investments and ideally the company is first to market. To an extent, competition can be good because it often validates emerging market segments; however, for our fund to make an investment, the company must exhibit a potential for market domination. A company's value is largely predicated on its ability to achieve technology/market advantage. We look very hard to find the unique aspect that makes this company an attractive opportunity and also try to identify its major risks and how they can be overcome/eliminated. Most of these companies in early markets require assumptions that must be evaluated for viability. Furthermore, (market) timing is a very critical element in early-stage investing; there are many examples where a company has been too early with its technology, product, or service and therefore failed. Finally and most importantly, a company's value will be determined by the strength, experience, and execution of the entrepreneur and its management team. When investing in markets, which are dynamic, it is critical to have management that is capable of building and motivating a great team and leading it effectively

Successful new business ideas can have many different characteristics, depending on the market situation. When access to capital is freer, it is much easier to support large and broad visions. In times where capital is scarce, people tend to demand results very early on (sometimes too early) – primarily revenue and profits – in a manner that supports long-term responsibility and growth. I believe a successful business idea is one that provides groundbreaking benefit while providing a rational and pragmatic strategy. The combination provides opportunities for companies to grow faster than their peers.

Venture capitalists are looking for a return that justifies their investment risk. Earlier stage funds will have a higher risk tolerance whereby there will be more failures, but the successes need to be very large (potentially a ten times return). VCs take into account that some companies will be total failures, which is the nature of our business. We also expect to have a couple of companies that are "dogs" – not total failures, but they also don't generate much return. Potentially, we expect to have one or two big winners in a portfolio of ten companies. Given the capital markets these days, this is a tough proposition because you have to manage to grow companies and conserve capital, while the opportunities for attractive exit opportunities (Initial Public Offering or Acquisition) are limited.

Taking Risks and Avoiding Missteps

Venture capitalists are required to assess and manage many risks to help make the investment successful. We try to identify the major risks such as technology, market, or management early on in the investment process, and structure the transaction accordingly so that our involvement and money helps to eliminate it. As a company progresses after our investment, we are constantly monitoring it, such as whether management is executing on its operating plan or whether the team needs to be augmented.

Entrepreneurs are independent thinkers who must press forward in spite of the many obstacles that usually arise. While this independence is positive overall, it can lead to management making rash decisions and mistakes. One mistake is that they often don't recognize when they need to ask for help. It is very important to surround entrepreneurs with experienced operators to help guide the company through difficult times. Another problem that we confront is when management fails to adapt to a changing marketplace and continues pursuing its original plan. Entrepreneurs tend to be optimists who feel as though they can affect every aspect of their business in spite of a changing market environment. The inflexibility to adapt to new circumstances can cause companies to fail very quickly. Ultimately I feel that people-related problems are the biggest risk in startup businesses. Building a great team and retaining and motivating it can make all the difference in building a great sustainable company.

It is also common for entrepreneurs to raise too much or too little money. In my experience, too much money can have an effect on a company's discipline; raising too little money on the other hand can affect a company's growth process. Especially in times of scarce capital, that management suffers significant distraction - often putting customers, partners, and operations on hold while in the fund-raising process. The ramifications could be hard to overcome. Our position is that in today's market – depending on which segment and the stage you're in – we prefer that companies be funded for 18 to 24 months. Entrepreneurs should look at milestones they want to reach in the specific funding period so in the future they can raise capital based on very clear results that they have delivered.

It is very common for venture capitalists to make similar mistakes as entrepreneurs. It is a VC's job to continuously monitor the progress and stage of the company to determine if the plan pursued is appropriate, and the management is capable of operating successfully in this market environment. The dynamics of operating within an early-stage technology market is that the margin of error for companies is very small.

VC Strategies

The decision making process is built on mutual consensus within the VC partnership. Given the small size of most VC firms, the most precious asset that we have is time. The decision to devote resources to a particular deal is not easy to make. The process arises out of internal discussions that the time spent learning about the new opportunity will be worthwhile and could lead to investment. Building a solid argument to pursue an investment opportunity requires a deep understanding of trends that are occurring (or bound to occur) in an industry. These trends are rarely definable at first glance. They require deep knowledge of markets and detailed discussions with many industry experts to augment that.

Deals are presented for investment decision only after we have completed an exhaustive due diligence of the technology, market, management, as well as financial and legal aspects. When early-stage deals are discussed internally, every partner typically remains very skeptical until they are convinced by presented facts and research to convince them that the prospect for significant returns is there.

Once we decide to invest, we tend to be very active participants. Our philosophy is that we only want to invest in companies where we can add significant value through our experience, relationships, and guidance. We typically request a seat on a company's Board of Directors, which provides us with the oversight necessary to manage our invested capital, while giving us accessibility to the company's decision-making process.

We expect management to provide us with the most current and credible information that they have regarding market trends, competition, financial, and growth strategies. The Board's responsibility is to process this information and make as strong an impact as possible. We devote significant time and attention to all portfolio companies. Our firm's rule of thumb is that we spend about 50 percent of our time with existing companies, and 50 percent with new opportunities that lay the foundation for our fund's future.

Entrepreneurs and venture capitalists spend years together working to build enterprise value for the company. As most venture funds have a certain lifecycle (typically ten years), over time we are working to achieve an exit from our holding in a company – with the goal of generating a significant return. Such an exit can be achieved by bringing a company public or by achieving a trade sale to another, most of the times, larger company. The backlash against the technology sector in recent years has forced companies to determine how they will grow most effectively. VCs cannot afford to continuously invest in companies that have little opportunity for high returns. Often tough decisions must be made whether a company should continue independently, be sold to a larger company with deeper pockets, or in the worst case be written off and liquidated entirely. These are not easy decisions to make. Personally, I find it most fulfilling for a company to make it standing alone. However, the downside risk must be considered to determine whether this route is a possibility that exists at any given time.

Trying to predict the future is a very humbling experience. It is the nature of venture capital that some companies fail. This can be a hurting experience. At the same time, failed ventures provide incredible experiences to learn and draw from to help future companies succeed.

Looking Forward

Our fund has developed key strategies to help increase our likelihood of success. We've implemented a strong internal process, and we have a very clear external market focus. With all the companies that are sent for us to evaluate, it is important that we don't stray too far away from focus. We've spent significant time and resources determining the market segment we want invest in, and we maintain our focus on these markets. Maintaining our industry knowledge is critical for our success, but it is also very difficult. Technology markets change so quickly that keeping up with companies, issues, and trends is an extremely demanding process.

Venture capital has up cycles and down cycles. Between 1996 and 2000, we had a very unique up cycle that seemingly defied gravity. We're clearly in a down cycle now. Fundamentally, today you have to be a little more realistic about success probabilities. By looking at the exit markets, it's obvious that there will be fewer companies that are going to make it. Valuations are going to be lower, so you must bid less capital for those companies and your entry valuation has to be lower as well. Successful companies in today's market have built themselves on strong fundamentals and steady growth; it takes at least five years to build a company from infancy until it is strong and sustainable. Entrepreneurs should not be discouraged by the market economy too much. There are many venture capital funds that have raised large sums of capital waiting to invest in the right opportunity.

The two main catalysts for venture capital success are corporate spending and exit markets, and both are in dire position these days. We are dependent on them to improve so that the industry will have more successes. It is extremely difficult to predict when outside market conditions will improve, but I believe if companies are grown correctly they can withstand these tough economic times. Our fund is fortunate to have a lot of cash on hand to invest, and we are excited about the quality of the new companies that we are evaluating. We believe that many companies from this market down cycle could be the drivers of tomorrow's economy.

I'm optimistic about the future. It's a great time to invest if you look at the long-term potential for success. It is no surprise that many of the technology high-fliers were built and funded during tough economic times. Investors that are active and engaged in those times can reap significant financial returns.

Fundamentally I'm very passionate about the venture capital profession. It's a fascinating business that places you in the middle of new trends and exposes you to some of the brightest people in the industry. The process of helping companies, from the early-stage concepts through the development of products and services that provide tangible value to customers, is extremely gratifying. I'm continually fascinated by the fusion of entrepreneurial drive and profound technology concepts that come together to create great companies or even industries.

Mathias Schilling is a Partner at Bertelsmann Ventures and a General Partner at BV Capital. He has been with BV since its inception in 1997 and served as a board member of several portfolio companies. Mathias has been instrumental in the setup of BV Capital and focuses on US investments in the areas of media, wireless, and software, primarily operating out of the San Francisco office of BV Capital. Prior to BV, he was employed by Bertelsmann AG as a consultant where he worked with Jan on the negotiation and execution of several joint venture and M&A transactions. Previous work experience also include Bertelsmann's Book Group in New York as well as the consultancy firm Roland Berger & Partner in Paris. He received his Master's degree in Finance from the University of St. Gallen in Switzerland.

Mastering the Fundamentals of Venture Capital

Terry McGuire

Polaris Venture Partners
Co-Founder, Managing General Partner

Recognizing Opportunity

Market opportunities often represent the convergence – sometimes unforeseen – of multiple trends. This convergence may result from a shift in the environment or from newly available technology. Whatever the cause, our job is to analyze what is taking place and ponder the question: "Where can this idea go?" Our answers are more likely to be accurate – and our investments more productive – if we analyze and invest in a number of non-competitive companies being launched around certain trends. At the same time we must develop a deep understanding of those industries and their customers.

The regulatory process can play an important role in evaluating opportunities, especially in life sciences. As venture capitalists, we're investing in partnerships with a life span of ten years. As such, we can't invest in a company that will take twenty years to produce a product. Ten years may sound like a long time. But it often takes three years for a company to get off the ground and another three to seven years before a product gets approved. Being able to anticipate the regulatory process is an important part of the investment decisions.

Evaluating a Company and its Business Model

The value of a company results from a combination of many factors: market opportunity, proprietary technology, defensible barriers, the ability to produce a profitable product with appropriate margins, and an acceptable rate of customer adoption. We evaluate a company's financing strategy because we know it takes a long time for companies to develop. Most important, we look at the management team. We try to determine if they have the skills required to develop products and assess whether they can weather the storms along the way.

Evaluating a business model also involves analyzing a variety of components: the value of a product, cost structures, pricing opportunities, and resulting margins. We have to understand the company's path to profitability. We also have to assess the market, and what favorable or hostile events are likely to take place that will affect the product's success. Part of this is understanding the company's customers. How quickly will they adopt the product? What is it about their practices that will accelerate or hinder product adoption?

Assuming the product will be adopted, we then have to ask if it can be produced. How long is it going to take? Again, answering this question involves understanding the regulatory environment. How big are the clinical trials? How long will they take? How much will they cost? Ultimately, we have to evaluate the financing strategy the company has in place to raise the capital required to get to an approved product.

With answers to these questions, we then need to assess the product's potential and, thereby, the enterprise value. Does it make sense to invest $50 million to launch a product destined to serve a population that will lead to a $100 million entity?

Finally, we evaluate the financial risks. Given that we manage a large portfolio, we're prepared to take a risk. Often we will structure our investments in order to mitigate risk, knowing there are some questions we simply can't answer until product trials begin.

Creating Partnerships with Entrepreneurs

Entrepreneurs should do as much homework, or due diligence, on venture capitalists as venture capitalists do on them. The goal is to determine whether the personalities fit – whether the personal style of the venture capitalist is an appropriate one for the entrepreneur. To find out, the entrepreneur should talk to others who have worked with the venture capitalist and ask how he or she behaved, not only in good situations, but in bad situations. Entrepreneurs should try to spend a lot of time with venture capitalists before they agree to take their capital. Entrepreneurs need to know what's going to happen in both good times and in difficult moments. They should test venture capitalists in any way they can to see if they behave like a good partner. I find it a huge disappointment if entrepreneurs do not perform due diligence on me. Who would enter a marriage without knowing their spouse-to-be? An entrepreneur who hasn't done his homework gives the impression of being naïve about the process of launching a business.

The set of relationships a venture capitalist brings to the partnership also is important. Has the venture capitalist done this before? Has he worked in a similar space? Does he have conflicting obligations in that space? Does he have a network of industry associates that will be helpful in launching the entrepreneur's product? The entrepreneur should answer these questions for himself.

Venture capitalists must do their homework as well. We should be testing our entrepreneurs and arriving at an intuitive understanding of how they operate in good times and bad. When trouble strikes – and trouble strikes every startup company – we want to know that the entrepreneur is going to be very candid, straightforward and creative about solving problems. Anything that leads me to believe that entrepreneurs may not be completely honest with me or, even worse, with themselves, is a big danger signal.

The word partner is the operative word. You have to approach a venture capital relationship as a partnership. If the entrepreneur finds that the venture capitalist is overpromoting the opportunity, overlooking the risks, or minimizing them in a flippant way, a red flag should go up. If the venture capitalist is not straightforward about what the risks and challenges are – or if he overplays the opportunities – that's a sign the venture capitalist hasn't done enough due diligence. Venture capitalists should be just as leery of entrepreneurs who minimize risks and maximize potential opportunities.

Our approach to investing is to keep a lot of capital in reserve for the rough places in the road. Trouble could show up in many different ways. If the technology doesn't work, we need to figure out if we can fix it or replace it. If the market turns out to be not very interesting, we need to find another one to approach. This requires creative problem solving. Blame is never an appropriate response when trouble appears.

The first approach to solving problems in a good partnership is to avoid blame and look together for creative solutions. We begin by asking, "How can we work together to solve this problem?" The second approach is to have enough intellectual integrity to admit that if a problem is not solvable within the constraints of time and capital, the best course is to withdraw. We sometimes conclude by saying, "This was a good idea, but it just isn't going to happen, so we all need to move on to something different."

In our experience, misjudging personal and professional compatibility is the most costly mistake made in venture capital relationships. Although it doesn't happen as much today, I've seen entrepreneurs simply take a term sheet because they liked the price. And I've seen other entrepreneurs take a lower term sheet because they liked the partner. If you asked me which cases worked out better, I would say the latter. Sometimes a good partner is willing to pay the highest price; that is a perfect world for the entrepreneur. But if I were an entrepreneur, I would definitely focus on the quality of the relationship, as opposed to the data on the term sheet.

Evaluating the Amount of Money a Company Needs

Entrepreneurs can raise either too little money or too much money. When they raise too little, they probably did not look at the run rate carefully enough, or they made faulty assumptions. Sometimes they want to take less dilution and own more of the company. Whatever the cause, they find they are running out of gas and are now in an awkward spot.

Entrepreneurs also can raise too much money, which presents dangers of a different kind. If they raise a large amount of capital and it is sitting in a bank account, the tendency is to spend it – but not necessarily on the right things. When entrepreneurs raise too much capital up front, the pre-money evaluation often is very high. As a result, the company might end up with a valuation it can't support. Some people put in more money than required up front but are still expecting to get a good return on it. The entrepreneur may end up with a lot of disappointed investors, because he took the money and, ultimately, was unable to deliver the goods.

Clearly, there are often issues of pricing an investment. However, the entrepreneur should put pricing in the perspective of the company's ultimate financial strategy. That means looking beyond the current financing round. Entrepreneurs should envision how much capital will be required to get to profitability, then work backward to determine how much capital should be raised in each round and at what price so that each round has gain in it.

The terms of a deal also are important, particularly in regard to issues of ownership and control. This goes to the heart of the partnership arrangement. Entrepreneurs need to ask themselves what they ultimately want to do with their companies. Early in my career, a wonderful entrepreneur came to see me one day, and I asked him what he wanted to do with his business. He told me he wanted to pass it on to his son. My comment was, "That's a wonderful goal. But it's not mine. My goal is to achieve some return, not to create a family business." In other words, entrepreneurs and venture capitalists need to be on the same page. The motivations of venture capitalists are fairly clear: we are interested with money from major institutions in order to produce a return for them (and for us). That almost always entails a liquidity event at some point. Entrepreneurs must understand their own motivations and make sure the terms of the transaction into which they are entering reflect those motivations.

Often entrepreneurs and venture capitalists get hung up on terms involving control. I've seen situations where the entrepreneur wants simply to take the capital without giving up any control. He doesn't want to treat the venture capitalist as a partner. I've seen other situations where the venture capitalist wants the entrepreneur to be a slave to the board. My personal preference is to avoid both of these extremes – to try to find a middle ground where it's recognized that everyone can make a contribution. Therefore I prefer to create a board that is balanced and not weighted toward one group or the other.

My strong advice is that new entrepreneurs obtain the input of experienced corporate counsel. Sometimes entrepreneurs will turn to lawyers who are their friends but who have never dealt with private equity before. It can be painful if both entrepreneurs and their corporate counsel are learning on the job. There are many strong law firms. If I was an entrepreneur, I'd want one that was experienced in this area of deal-making.

Understanding Trends in the Industry

Through the late 1990s, syndication – the participation of several firms in a deal – went out of favor, particularly on the IT side. Venture capitalists were trying to grab as much of a deal as they possibly could. Sometimes this turned out to be a hollow victory, if you were left standing alone with a company in trouble. Now syndication is back in style.

The most obvious benefit of having multiple firms in a funding round is the amount of capital and reserve available. In addition, as a venture capitalist, I find it helpful to have at least one other partner whose interests are purely in line with my own. If such a co-investor sees a different set of problems, or takes a different approach, I don't have to worry about his motivation. It's particularly helpful to have co-investors with whom you've been in the trenches before, both in good times and bad.

A more important paradigm shift involves layers of financing. In the pre-1995 era, there were seed investors at the very early stages, then first-round investors, second-round investors, and mezzanine investors. Each investor stage was relying on the next one to support it. That has gone away. Today, a venture capitalist has to be a cradle-to-grave investor. We have to be in every round, not just the first. As a result, having co-investors from the beginning is very important. Companies require continual feeding to achieve their ultimate goals: to produce important products and achieve strong profitability.

Despite today's tough climate, I think only great things lie in store. Markets go up and down, but technology does not. There is a major transformation taking place in IT. When I look at my household and my business, I find both are spending more money on IT today than ever before. Information technology is only going to become more and more important.

In life sciences, the door is just beginning to open. Consider biotech and the genomics revolution. The idea of turning an empirical science into an engineering science – systems biology – is just beginning to evolve. It will create huge opportunities with rich rewards.

Certainly, there will be short-term swings up and down. Some venture firms will be started and some will fail. The challenge of this business is negotiating short-term difficulties to capitalize on long-term trends. But the fundamentals are excellent. There are more experienced venture capital teams today than there have ever been. There are more experienced entrepreneurs. There is more capital, more technology, and more markets willing to take on new products. In many ways, this is the best of times, but it's not without challenging moments. Clearly, 2000-

2002 has been a particularly difficult timeframe for technology companies everywhere.

Advice

I started my venture capital career with a firm called Golder, Thoma and Cressey in Chicago. Stan Golder was my mentor. I remember Stan often saying that lemons mature faster than pearls. Ours is a long-term business. Venture funds are ten-year partnerships. For whatever reason, companies that are not meant to be successful show up earlier than the ones that will succeed. As venture capitalists, we have to deal with the lemons before we benefit from the pearls.

Another good piece of advice comes from Jean Deleage at Alta Partners. Jean is a big believer in doing lots of penetrating due diligence, but ultimately he recognizes that venture capital is an intuitive business. That makes it an apprenticeship business as well. Developing an intuition for what is going to work requires exposure to many great entrepreneurs (and many unsuccessful entrepreneurs), many greats deals (and many mediocre ones), many promising new technologies (and many that fail to deliver). This takes time; it can't happen overnight. Even when a venture capitalist has done his homework and studied all the objective data carefully, investment decisions boil down to gut reactions. Stan Golder said it in a slightly different way: venture capitalists use four parts of their bodies – their minds, hearts, guts, and the seat of their pants. The last three have nothing to do with quantitative analysis. You have to develop a sense for a deal.

The rules for success in venture capital are basically the same as for a successful marriage. Be honest and candid. Assume goodwill, common goals, and the need to find the middle ground to solve problems and reach the right solutions. Don't spend all your money at once. Be prepared to support your companies through the longer term.

To an entrepreneur, I would say hire great teams. Recognize that most entrepreneurs are appropriate for one stage in a company's development, but not the next. Entrepreneurs and venture capitalists are shareholders. What is good for the entire entity is good for both.

Terry McGuire is a co-founder and managing general partner based in Boston. Along with Steve Arnold and Jon Flint, he founded Polaris in 1996. Terry focuses on investments in the life sciences. Prior to starting Polaris, Terry spent seven years at Burr, Egan, Deleage & Co. investing in early stage medical and information technology companies. Terry began his career in venture capital at Golder, Thoma and Cressey in Chicago.

Terry has co- founded three companies: Inspire Pharmaceuticals (www.inspirepharm.com), AIR (Advanced Inhalation Research, Inc.), and MicroCHIPS (www.mchips.com). Terry represents Polaris on the boards of directors of Acusphere (www.acusphere.com), Remon (www.remonmedical.com) deCODE (www.decode.com), Microbia (www.microbia.com), MicroCHIPS (www.mchips.com), Transform Pharmaceuticals (www.transformpharma.com), and Wrenchead (www.wrenchead.com).

Terry has been elected to the boards of directors at both the Massachusetts Biotechnology Council (the leading trade organization of Massachusetts biotech and pharmaceutical companies) and MassMedic (the leading trade organization of Massachusetts medical device manufacturers). He has also been on the boards of Akamai (www.akamai.com), Cubist Pharmaceuticals (www.cubist.com), and Aspect Medical Systems (www.aspectmedical.com). Other Board seats include: the Thayer School of Engineering, Dartmouth College; the Foster Center for Private Equity at the Amos Tuck School, Dartmouth College; and the Whitehead Institute for Biomedical Research.

Terry holds an MBA from Harvard Business School, an MS in engineering from The Thayer School at Dartmouth College and a BS in physics and economics from Hobart College.

Venture Investing at Venrock

Anthony Sun

Venrock Associates
Co-CEO, Managing General Partner

Identifying Promising Early-Stage Companies

Opportunity comes in many ways. Our best opportunities come to us from the personal networks of Venrock's investment professionals. We have many entrepreneurs who have been successful with us in the past and they tend to be individuals who identify emerging markets or product opportunities. They come back to advise us. Also, there are broad trends that occur when there are fundamental breakthroughs in technology. For example, in the past when microprocessors came onto the scene, the personal computer industry was born. So we could extrapolate from one innovation and take some risks to see what the offspring of that innovation might be. This was the case when we made a founding investment in Apple Computer. From there it didn't take a leap of faith to realize that tools to make computers more useful, such as application software, would be valuable. Then a need for data storage emerged, spawning the disk drive industry. It is an evolutionary process where we look for opportunities at every step. Our healthcare partners are on top of the research being done at the major universities in the country, and they see fundamental signs and breakthroughs happening there. They look for opportunity in spinouts to commercialize these scientific breakthroughs.

We generally look at a variety of criteria when valuing a company. We look at market size, the solution that is addressing the market, whether there is an opportunity for rapid growth, and whether there's potential for a reasonably sized market. Second, we look very carefully at the people – the team, the entrepreneurs – what their experience and attitude are, as well as their domain expertise in the field that they are working in. Third, we look at the technology, and this is where our strength comes in – we are high-tech investors. Obviously there has to be a clear technology differentiation in the opportunity. It has to offer a magnitude of improvement over existing solutions in order to make it worthwhile to take the risk. A standard rule of thumb is that it gives ten times better price/performance, and that it solves quantifiable customer pain. Finally, we look at the deal economics. Does the opportunity have a reasonable capital requirement? Is there a large enough market opportunity to build a stand-alone company?

Company Valuation and Expected Returns

Valuation is an art and not a science. It varies according to market comparables. If you look at the average values of deals in 1995-2000, they all went up because the exit values also went up. But as the market came back down to reality in late 2000, the values adjusted accordingly. We have certain rules of thumb regarding what an opportunity is worth based on the stage at which we are investing, what we are investing in, what sector the company is in, how complete the team is, and what the opportunity for a liquidity event looks like down the road. Given all of these factors, our partnership comes to some consensus as to what the appropriate valuation should be for the opportunity involved.

It's very hard to nail down exactly what kind of growth criterion these companies must meet for us to be interested in the opportunity. These are very early-stage companies with no existing cash flow and highly variable financial plans. The internal criterion we use, the simple rule of thumb, is that we need a return of five times our invested capital in the period of five to seven years. If you look at what that entails, it requires the company to have a liquidity event – they need to be either merged out or they need to have a successful public offering. Our usual exercise is to work with the entrepreneurs to build an operating plan for the company that reflects product development costs, sales timing expectations and other factors, and then compare this to expected exit scenarios.

Venture capitalists value companies differently than public equities analysts because the latter have a lot of data to work with. When we invest it's in the early stages of a startup; there are no earnings and projections are quite variable. We spend much more time looking at issues other than just pure financial performance. We have no way of using discounted cash flow models, or other quantitative analytics other professionals have when they invest in public entities. There are no multiples like price/earning ratios to evaluate. We really take the time to evaluate some of the subjective factors so that we can then triangulate into an evaluation.

Critical Factors in a Venture's Success

Experience counts when it comes to management. You need to have domain expertise, but your past experience in a successful entrepreneurial environment is very important. You need to have a demonstrated track record of success, an attitude that you will do whatever it takes to win, and fire in the belly to really want to work hard in difficult situations to build a successful company. It also doesn't hurt for the entrepreneur to have relationships with individuals who could be influencers, partners or customers in a given field.

We evaluate new entrepreneurs based upon their experience, their domain expertise in the field they want to enter, whether they have had any startup experience, and whether they have shown a demonstrated track record of success in their past work. Attitude is also very important.

Not all decisions or choices we make are successful, and that's why we play a very active role in the companies we invest in. If we sense that the entrepreneur is failing because of a lack of ability in certain functional areas, we help him to recruit complementary people to make up for the deficiencies.

The business model is also critical to the venture's success. Business models are evolving all the time, but the fundamentals never change. First of all, you have to be sure that the product or service can be sold at a price that generates a positive gross margin. Ultimately, the company must sustain enough operating margins that returns are profitable. Every time we violate those fundamental principles we do so to our detriment. There was a time during the dot-com boom when people were talking about new business models where growth and revenues were more important than becoming profitable. That was only during the go-go years; eventually, if you don't make a profit you go out of business.

Assessing Risks

There are several different kinds of risks in a deal. Clearly that includes people risk. The majority of our failures resulted when the entrepreneurs did not execute on their plan or because they did not have the experience to know what was required. To mitigate that risk, we spend a lot of time with entrepreneurs to get comfortable with them. We also do a lot of due diligence and reference checking to make sure that they are upstanding individuals, and even then that's the biggest failure point in all our investing history.

Then there are three other kinds of risk that we try to mitigate. One is market risk, and we do a lot of due diligence to make sure that the customers are there and that the industry is sound, but sometimes we are caught with the wrong timing. For instance, today the telecom industry is in a downward spiral, and therefore our telecom portfolio is suffering from the market risks; the customers have gone away.

The second risk is technology risk. This risk is that the entrepreneurs are attempting too much, and they cannot develop the product in a timely fashion within the budgets that are allocated, or that the science is too difficult and it turns out to be a failure. We are very good at evaluating those risks – those are less of an issue for us, but nonetheless it's a type of risk that we confront all of the time.

Finally, there is the financial risk, which is that sometimes it takes too much money to get a deal off the ground. For example, companies who sought to compete with the incumbent local telephone service providers did not anticipate the full cost of delivering highly reliable telephone service. A number of competitive and technology barriers left many competitive local exchange carriers (CLECs) with minimal cash flows, yet major capital requirements to service customers. In such cases, the risk-reward ratio breaks down.

Due Diligence and the VC's Role

Venture firms generally ask an entrepreneur about the issues that address the risk factors mentioned above. First question: Tell us about yourself. What's your background? Why do you want to do this? What motivates you? What are your past successes? We get to know them as best as we can. Then we generally ask them to explain to us in a simple presentation how their opportunity mitigates some of those risks. Then we will make an assessment as to whether or not it is a deal worth pursuing.

From the entrepreneur's point of view, they also have to make sure the interpersonal relationship works. Just as we spend time getting to know them they should spend time getting to know us. When you get involved with a company, it is for a minimum of three to five years, and there isn't any good way to divorce yourself once your money is invested. Likewise, the entrepreneurs need to know that the venture investors are people that they want to be associated with for that period of time, for better or for worse. The entrepreneurs need to get to know the potential investors. They also need to go and ask questions of previous venture portfolio CEOs about how we behave, what our expectations are, and how we deal with adversity, because that will help them to decide which venture firm best suits them.

Venrock takes a very active role when investing. We typically have a board seat on all of our portfolio companies. Our value as an investor is highest at the earliest stages of a company because we spend a lot of time with management in terms of helping them set the company's strategy, helping open doors to potential customers, service providers, channel partners, and so on. We introduce them to lenders, investment banks, industry leaders, consultants, and attorneys. We evaluate their plans and tactics, and we provide advice on a day-to-day basis as requested by the CEO. Generally we are known as coaches for the CEOs. As they run their businesses and encounter issues, we are a sounding board. Lastly, we help the company raise future rounds of capital. So we are a full-service investor. We work hard at staying current in technology and connected in industry so that, ideally, we can make a major impact on our companies.

We also ask the tough questions. We challenge the company to prove that the cash flow and the projections make sense. Are the development milestones on track? Will the customers still be in line when the product or service is available? We challenge their assumptions. We confirm that the entrepreneur's assumptions are valid and that they are still relevant in order to make sure that their business model stays on track. Those are challenges that sometimes the entrepreneurs take for granted. The benefit here is that company management has an outside perspective to inform decisions and a fresh perspective to enliven internal debates.

Changes in the Investment Industry

The last few years have been unique in the venture industry in that too much money came into the industry. If you look at the amount of capital that has come into the venture industry over the last few years, a decade ago it was about $2 billion and two years ago it was $200 billion, or 100 times more money coming into the industry. The whole industry has matured and that has changed how we look at the business. It is back to basics. We try to make sure that we are diversified as a fund. We invest in healthcare, in information technology, and in the telecom industry. We are diversified geographically, in California and in Boston, all over the United States. We make sure that we stick to our principles of investing with entrepreneurs and make sure that the business model really works. That is in contrast to other funds that were classified as momentum investors; they would invest when the market was moving up, and when the market was moving down, they would not, and that's a very short-term strategy.

The industry will consolidate. Clearly there is too much money in the industry, and there are too many professionals who came into the industry without a lot of experience. This is an industry where the mentorship model still works. A venture capitalist needs many years of experience before he or she can be successful. The industry grew too quickly. As the industry consolidates, we think it will go back to best practices and doing business the old-fashioned way, with some new twists.

Advice and Rules for Success

The best piece of venture capital advice I received is that this is a long-term process. There are no get-rich-quick deals out there. If you want to be successful, you have to create value, and to create value you have to build successful companies. That's the same advice I give all the time because when venture capitalists cut corners and think that they can cut the time frame it takes to be successful, and that is usually when they make the wrong decisions.

There are certain dynamics in a venture capital partnership that engender longevity. One is that there has to be good leadership. The leadership of the firm is important; it sets the culture and the tone. Second, there should be good mentorship, as the leaders pass down their knowledge, experience, and best practices to the younger partners. Third, there should be a good succession plan that allows younger partners the opportunity to grow, so that when the senior partners retire there are experienced and successful younger partners to take over the partnership. That's on the human side of the venture partnerships.

On the strategy side, you have to make sure that the firm has a strategy for the long-term. It has to have a strategy that looks out a decade or more and therefore forces it to be diversified, both in terms of geography and sector focus, and not to be chasing the latest hot fad – because when that hot fad is done you may end up with not much of a practice. Clearly, two years ago it was very faddish to be an Internet fund. Today an Internet-only fund will have difficult time surviving. The ability of a partnership to evolve its sector focus and expertise is essential to enduring success.

Finally, the golden rule for successful venture capitalist partnerships is to remember that our success is based on the success of our entrepreneurs. We often say internally that one of the more important measures of a venture firm's success is the extent to which our entrepreneurs seek us for the second or third time they want to start a business. The power of these relationships and trust transcend the size of the fund or popular view of which firms may be in vogue. As I said above, this is a long-term process, and a hallmark of successful venture firms is a philosophy of hard work and patience.

Anthony Sun is managing general partner and co-CEO of Venrock Associates, a venture capital fund associated with the Rockefeller Family office in New York. Venrock has offices in New York, Menlo Park and Cambridge. He invests primarily in the Information Technology Industry with a focus on the Communications and Internet infrastructure sectors.

Since joining Venrock in 1979, he has been instrumental as a lead investor or board member in over two dozen companies that have completed public offerings or successful mergers. He is a Managing General Partner of Venrock. His previous experience was with Hewlett-Packard, TRW and Caere Corporation. He currently sits on the boards of numerous companies in the Venrock portfolio.

Anthony is currently a Commissioner and Trustee of the Asian Art Museum of San Francisco where in the past he held positions of Vice

Chairman and member of the executive committee. He is a member of the board of the steering committee for the California Research Center of the Harvard Business School. Tony is also a member of the Corporation and Trustee of MIT, serving concurrently on the investment committee and visiting committees of the Department of Electrical Engineering and Computer Science and the Department of Material Science.

He is a key member of the Capital Campaign committee of the Jasper Ridge Biological Preserve of Stanford University and a member of the Stanford Associates. Since 1993, Anthony has been a Venture Capital Guest Advisor to the Stanford Business School Entrepreneurial Course.

Lastly, Anthony is a board member of the National Venture Capital Association and a member of the International Resource Panel for the Government of Singapore. He holds a B.S., M.S. and an advanced Engineer degree from MIT and an MBA from Harvard Business School.

Choosing the Right Investment

Lawrence E. Mock, Jr.
Mellon Ventures, Inc.
President & CEO

Assessing Investment Opportunities

Ultimately, a business opportunity develops because there is a problem that needs to be solved. An entrepreneur is often someone that is in the unique position of having experienced the pain associated with this problem and wants to do something to fix it. For example, there are a lot of us are roaming around town and country with computers, experiencing the pain of not being able to get connected. So wireless technology is something that we recently invested in. Similarly, on the business front, companies that manage large numbers of SKUs have an increasing need to do that and to present it in an online format, so that it goes beyond a paper catalogue and even an online catalogue. In SKU management, we have an investment in a company with a software product that addresses this particular problem that IT professionals need solved.

In terms of choosing a business to invest in, the first question we ask ourselves is why we want to be in this industry. We ask the entrepreneur to describe their industry and their business, and articulate why, if we have capital to invest, we would want to invest in it. If it's an early-stage company, we are typically one of a couple of venture capital groups that invest. We tend to make enough of an initial investment that we are on the board, and we own a significant portion of the company so that the time we spend with the company, if it's successful, is justified. In a later-stage company, we may own a majority of the company, and we may have two or three seats on the board. If not, we are probably appointing a couple of those seats. In either case, we like to have additional capital in reserve so that we can own more of our successful companies, albeit at higher prices.

One of the key indicators we use of future success is past success. That obviously equates to experience. We look at executives who also have personal characteristics beyond their professional experience. Those would include commitment to the business, tenacity, and integrity. We look at their economic commitment, as reflected either by their willingness to invest previously or their willingness to invest alongside us.

Company Valuation

In evaluating a new company, at least initially, we start with the management and their description of their business. This description should address their own industry dynamics and the nature of their product and their competition. If a presentation can't answer these fundamental questions, we're probably not interested in the company. If it does, it probably also gives us a good road map for some independent verification as to what industry trends and valuations are. Also, we have 130 portfolio companies so it's not unusual that we have some expertise within our portfolio CEOs to help us with this. We'll loop them into the equation. We also use all the usual published resource material, such as Forrester and Gartner.

In terms of simply looking at the financials, we do it line by line. We look at the revenue line, the historic performance of the company to see if the revenue forecast appears reasonable. If a company has been growing at 15 percent annually and all of a sudden it is assuming 50 percent growth, we'd want to know what had changed. That will drive questions at the revenue line. At the gross margin line, it depends on what kind of a product or service the company provides, but we will look at how they build up their cost, and we will compare that to other companies in the same industry. If you saw a distribution company with

60 percent gross margins, it would raise the question as to how they were able to be double or triple the margins of other distribution companies. On the expense line, which gets you down to operating income, we look at how they construct their sales and distribution expense and how much overhead is assumed. Finally, we look at whether their organizational structure is appropriate for the growth they expect going forward. Then, and probably most importantly at that level, we go back and look at how they sell. If it takes a direct sales force to sell a $5,000 product, you will need a lot of salesmen before you get to a significant level of revenue. If they are not developing indirect methods of sales or channel partners, it will affect their expenses and ultimately their ability to achieve sustained profitability. In terms of assessing growth in a later-stage company, we are probably looking at the 5 to 10 percent range. An earlier-stage company that can't demonstrate the potential to grow at least 20 percent is probably not going to be attractive, since it is starting with such a small base. One dollar compounded by 20 percent takes a long time to get to $100 million, whereas a $40 million company compounded by 10 percent doesn't take nearly as long.

The best thing for an entrepreneur who has never evaluated a term sheet is to get an experienced legal professional to help them. There is a lot of detail on a term sheet, and if you are not familiar with it, then it might as well be written in a foreign language. The venture capital industry tends to operate in a very systematic way, so you would want to make sure that the appropriate terms are in the term sheet and that they are within normal boundaries. With more conventional terms, I'd get a good lawyer to help. There are only two other issues regarding the term sheet. One is pricing, and the other is choosing the best partner. The first is as much art as science, and the latter may ultimately be the most important decision an entrepreneur makes.

Valuation

We're in the business of taking risks. If you're taking a risk, it implies that on occasion you are going to fail. If the venture capital industry has for the last 20 years returned an average of 15 percent annually to its investors, then on an early-stage deal if we're not making 40 to 50 percent annually, we are probably not going to end up with a portfolio that returns 15 percent because that is the level of risk inherent in a venture capital portfolio. One way that you deal with risk is that you price accordingly. The way you assess the risk comes back to the stage of the company, the quality of the management, how much they have penetrated their market, and whether or not you can accurately assess the market demand for the product.

In determining the value of a company, we look at three things. The first is whether or not they have a product or service that provides long-term sustainable customer value. Second, we look at whether they have an economic business model – in other words, can they sell their product or service at a profit? And third, we look at the ability of the management team to execute the plan that they are presenting.

In evaluating an earlier-stage company, we tend to look at how much money has been invested in it previously, how much money it needs to complete its plan, and how much of the business we would have to own so if they accomplish their business plan we get an adequate return for our investors. That said, early stage companies today tend to price at to a single-digit valuation – a million, two million, up to nine million.

A startup requires huge amounts of capital. As it develops a revenue base, it becomes a little bit easier to value because we can look at either fractions of or multiples of their revenue. This technique, too, is not an exact science. Should we look at yesterday's, today's, or tomorrow's revenue base? As the company develops an income stream, valuation becomes easier because we look at comparable companies and the earnings multiples at which they trade. There are benchmarks for every industry, but you would have to know, for example, that credit card processing tends to trade at one-and-a-half to two times revenue and six times operating cash flow. The art comes into what number you apply that multiple to – whether it is yesterday, today, or tomorrow. You go back to the quality of the product or service and the ability of the management team to execute. This gives a very broad range, but it is done typically in a negotiation and even in a competitive process. The last and final check is that the market tends to speak. Just like there are changes in demand for any product or service, this is also true for capital and particularly for venture capital. Right now, venture capital tends to be scarce and therefore fairly expensive. Going back two years, it tended to be abundant and relatively cheap.

In 1996, I read a quote from one of the partners at Sequoia who said – and I'm paraphrasing – that he didn't know how many good ideas there were in the world, but he knew $1 billion could fund every one of them. Since there were tens of billions of dollars within five miles of his office, 90 percent of the money was probably going to be lost. The trend you've seen in the last few years is that when those billion dollars of ideas develop, they need additional money to expand and capitalize on their market potential. You've seen the venture capital industry in the last couple of years move toward that second stage of financing. This is probably healthy for the industry, and it is probably where the best outcomes occur. Prices will go up in later-stage deals, and consequently the returns will go down. Funding those billion dollars of ideas will become attractive again. This is the natural cycle of venture capital.

Mistakes of Entrepreneurs

The biggest mistake entrepreneurs make is demonstrating a lack of realism about their market. You see that reflected in financial statements for startups that project revenues of $100 million at the end of two years; life is just not that easy. Building a substantial business enterprise takes more time and more money than is often appreciated. If an entrepreneur is unrealistic about this, in all likelihood he or she will not end up with a successful new enterprise. Also, if a person is completely naive about the way the venture capital or professional equity investor marketplace works, it is going to be difficult to work with that person going forward. Just to give a quick example, virtually all venture capital investments today are in preferred stock, which effectively means that particularly if a deal isn't working, the person who puts in the capital gets the money back first. Is that a debatable term? Sure, everything is debatable, but since 99 percent of the deals done today involve preferred stock, if we run into an entrepreneur who is dogmatic in resisting that term, we are probably going to have trouble with him or her on other things. I think it is important for an entrepreneur to be fairly well schooled in how the capital marketplace works.

To be successful in approaching a venture capital firm, you need to find some direct connection to it. It can be personal or professional. Most venture firms now post their portfolios on their websites. If you had a wireless software product, for example, you could go to our website and see that we've invested in a wireless software company called Nomadix.

Since we are organized into practice groups, you could contact one of the professionals that it falls under. You could look up the person who is on the board of Nomadix and call or email that person and say, "I know you are involved in Nomadix, and I've got a similar product or service." If you wanted to be really inventive, you could go to the Nomadix CEO and say, "I've got a product that doesn't compete with yours but is addressing problems in the same industry." Obviously the guy will get engaged with what it is, and at the end you can ask, "Could you introduce me to the guy at Mellon Ventures that financed you?" That is a professional approach. On the personal side, we are all members of associations and groups, alumni organizations, entrepreneurial networks, and so on. Working one of those contacts would make sense, but just coming in cold, either by email or by direct mail, your probabilities of success are extremely low. You've got to have a hook.

Ideal Liquidation Scenarios

My opinion is that the ideal liquidation scenario – and I'm speaking here of early-stage investments – is for a much bigger company to see the potential of the product or service that the company is delivering and to recognize that the company does not have the resources to obtain the full potential on its own. They come in and pay cash for the company. They are valuing it on the basis of what they can do with it. Coca-Cola just bought a soft drink company on the West Coast – a little company that made exotic fruit juices. It wasn't going to be able to penetrate the world market in the lifetime of its founders, but Coca-Cola already has penetrated the world market. By running the new product through the Coca-Cola distribution system, Coke makes a lot of money. In that case, they are willing to pay a huge amount for the company despite the fact that it is still a small company with limited internal growth prospects.

The second-best scenario is if you've got one of those one-in-a-million ideas, and simply by applying additional capital you can reach full potential. A public offering then makes sense. I think the venture industry and the entrepreneurs got those backward over the last couple of years. Going public was viewed as everyone's ideal outcome when in fact the people who did the best through that period were the ones who sold out to bigger companies who needed their products or services.

Advice for Venture Capitalists

The best thing an institutional venture capitalist can do is read everything that is published, whether it is electronic or paper-based. Another is to get out of the office – good deals are found in the field, not behind your desk. Finally, I would not invest with somebody that you are not completely comfortable with, both personally and professionally. I would not only pass this on to venture capitalists, I would pass it on to entrepreneurs. If you're not personally and professionally comfortable with your venture capitalist, you probably ought to find another one.

The number-one rule in venture capital is that, ultimately, success depends upon creating value. That is, creating value within your portfolio company. In turn, it is important that the portfolio company create value at the customer level. It is easy for financially oriented people to get distracted by structural gimmicks, but ultimately, at the end of the day it comes down to customer value at the portfolio company level and value creation at the venture capital level. Rule number two is that management matters and experience counts. Third, this business is substance over form, and not the reverse. In the last couple of years, the form of the transaction – the structure – has taken precedence over the substance; this really gets you back to rule one. Rule number four is that this is an industry that is rewarded over the long-term, so a long-term perspective is required. Therefore, integrity and reputation matter. A fifth rule would be that because we are privileged to be in one of the most exciting businesses around today, we ought to appreciate it and have some fun.

The most exciting thing about being in venture capital is seeing a portfolio company succeed. I have often said that it is a lot like a parent watching a child get married. Everybody feels good about the situation, and while there is some apprehension about the future, seeing a portfolio company succeed is a lot like watching a child succeed. Then they leave. To the extent that you feel like you contributed to their success, you ought to be satisfied.

Lawrence Mock is President and CEO of Mellon Ventures, Inc., Mellon Financial Corporation's private equity investment business. Through Mellon Ventures LP, Mellon invests across the venture capital spectrum, providing rapidly growing operating companies and superior management teams with access to the capital necessary to fuel their ambitious business plans. Begun in 1996, Mellon Ventures has invested in or committed over $1.3 billion in capital to over 130 operating businesses and 50 venture capital funds. About 1/3 of the companies it has backed have subsequently gone public or been sold.

Previously Mr. Mock was President of River Capital, Inc., an Atlanta-based venture capital firm that he and three partners founded in 1983. River invested over $200 million of debt and equity in companies throughout the Southeast. During this period, Mr. Mock served as Chairman of three companies, including one listed on the American Stock Exchange, and was a director of 14 other River-affiliated and unaffiliated companies, both public and private. During his tenure, River Capital's return on investment placed it near the top of the U.S. venture capital industry. Prior to River Capital, Mr. Mock was chief operating officer of a $100 million aviation sales, service and distribution company with over 1,000 employees in fifteen locations. The company was sold to a Raytheon subsidiary in 1983 for a record industry multiple. He was also a senior manager of Fuqua Industries, a diversified Fortune 500 company, and an Associate with Booz, Allen & Hamilton.

Mr. Mock has served as an officer and director of many non-profit business and community organizations. He chaired the Society of International Business Fellows and the Atlanta International School during their periods of rapid change and growth. He is currently a Trustee of the Pressley Ridge Schools, a non-profit institution with a $60 million annual budget serving troubled and troubling children and Sewickley Academy, an independent school serving a tri-state area. He served as a US Delegate to the United Nations and as a White House Fellow.

Mr. Mock is currently a member of the World Presidents Organization and the Chief Executives Organization. He received a bachelor's degree from Harvard College, a master's degree from Florida State University, and completed his postgraduate education at the London School of Economics.

Successfully Evaluating Opportunities

Michael Carusi

Advanced Technology Ventures
General Partner

Finding Value

I invest in healthcare companies. More specifically, I focus on medical devices and biotechnology. Within these sectors, there are very clear metrics to measure value. These metrics are particularly important, given the fact that most of these companies do not have revenues or cash flows. When I first evaluate an opportunity, I always lead with the people. A stronger management team always means more value. I also evaluate the technical founders, the scientific advisors, the business advisors, and the existing Board Members. Again, quality begets quality and therefore value. It is a cliché, but I would rather invest in an "A" management team with a "B" technology than in an "A" technology with a "B" team. The better team always wins.

After the team, I look at the unmet need and market potential of the product the company is developing. As a general rule, large markets with high unmet needs prevail. Within healthcare, this typically means U.S. markets typically in excess of $1 billion. High unmet needs refer to diseases with high morbidity, i.e. people who are disabled or high mortality. High unmet needs always trump large markets. I would rather invest in a company targeting a small, but fatal disease with a life saving device than a company targeting a large, but well served disease with a device which only provides incremental improvements.

The team, market potential, and unmet needs only represent the first set of screening criteria. Once these hurdles are met, I then evaluate the next set of screens. These include intellectual property, competitive position, time to market, regulatory requirements, and capital needs. All of these factors are measured against risk. Higher risk requires higher upside.

Lastly, I gauge value by evaluating the company's stage. If it is a medical device company and their ultimate goal is to get a product to market, I attempt to peg their progress. Are they engineering and developing the product? Is the product in human studies? Is the product safe? Effective? Does the company have FDA approval? Are they out selling the product? Are they generating revenues? Are they profitable? As a company progresses along this continuum, the more their value increases. The closer to market, the lower the risk, and therefore the higher the value.

Management Team

I always start with the CEO. It is always nice to have a strong CEO in place. To me, a strong CEO is a person who has done it before. A person who has run a small company, created value in that company, and seen his or her way to a successful exit, be it an IPO or acquisition. It is a person who is entrepreneurial and knows how to be capital efficient. Big company managers are very talented, but they do not always make the best small company CEOs. Often, there is a lack of urgency. A need to create a beurocracy, rather than creating a well-functioning, nimble organization. The best combination is an individual who spent their early years at a big company and then transitioned to a startup. A big company brings functional skills, a small company brings passion. Management skills are not the only benchmark of success. Domain expertise is also essential. A person may have been a successful CEO before, but I would be concerned if they come from a different industry. I am looking for a combination of track record, leadership skills, experience, and relevant domain expertise. Often a tall order to fill.

Lastly, the individual must fit the stage of the company. A company will often transition through two or three CEOs as it grows and moves towards commercialization. This is natural and healthy. For example, if a company is early in product development, an individual who is strong technically may be appropriate. If the company is generating revenues, an individual with strength in sales and marketing may be appropriate. The rules are not steadfast, each company is different.

The team begins with the CEO, but it certainly does not end there. The organization will make or break the company. This includes both structure and dynamics. A team needs to be well-balanced functionally, but it also needs to be well-balanced socially. A poorly functioning team will kill an organization. A good CEO can influence these dynamics, but the wrong mix of individuals can be hard to overcome. Like the CEO, the composition of the team depends on the stage of the company. A strong VP of Engineering is essential for product development, a strong VP Clinical and Regulatory is essential to execute on a clinical trial, and a strong VP Sales and Marketing is necessary to generate revenues. These individuals do not need to be on board from day one. In fact, many times they are not. However, these individuals must be brought on as the company progresses.

Despite my desire for a strong organization, a management team often has holes. It would not be an early-stage company if it did not. In fact, there are times when a company does not even have a CEO. It may simply consist of a few technical founders. This is not unexpected, but it does affect value. Without question, the risk is higher if the team is incomplete. This also means the company will require more of my time personally. Nine times out of ten, I will take a board seat when I invest in a company. This is true for most early-stage venture capitalists. By and large, venture investors tend to be active board members. Board meetings are typically held 6-8 times per year. A good director will serve as a sounding board to the management team and provide another point of view. This point of view is often more cynical than that of the team's. A director's job is to challenge and dig, not rubber stamp. Venture capitalist directors question strategies, question plans and question spending. As a director, I want to understand and get comfortable with the thinking of the team.

Most venture capitalists have operating backgrounds rather than finance backgrounds. This means we have been in the trenches and have the battle scars to prove it. It also means we have made mistakes in the past. Hopefully we have learned from these mistakes and can pass this learning on to our entrepreneurs. We are not there to be micromanagers. We are not there to become involved in the day-to-day business of the company. In fact, if a board is doing these things, it is usually a signal that the wrong CEO is in place.

Approaches

The first thing an entrepreneur needs to do is to take a hard look at their company and be realistic. Is the company early-stage or later-stage? Should it be venture backed? Is the company likely to provide the upside most venture capitalists require, and, more importantly, is the entrepreneur willing to give up some level of control? These questions need to be answered in advance of the fund raising process. If the upside is not there or expectations on control are not realistic, the company will not get funded.

Once the self-analysis is complete, the entrepreneur can begin to search for the appropriate venture capitalist or private equity investors. Different firms invest in different stages. Some venture capitalists define themselves as early-stage investors while others prefer later-stage opportunities. The trick for the entrepreneur is to match the stage of their company with the right group. If it is a Series A or Series B investment, look for an early-stage investor. If it is a biotechnology company, look for a healthcare investor. If it is a software company, look for an IT investor.

The best thing an entrepreneur can do to identify the appropriate investors is to network. This will be the key to life in a startup. Talk to other entrepreneurs, talk to other CEOs, and talk to other folks who are out raising money. Find out who they know, who they have worked with, and who they like and trust. Conferences and websites can also provide insight into the types of investor who are out there. Ultimately, however, personal relationships will provide the best reference to a firm. Entrepreneurs should use these relationships for introductions. I have never invested in a company that has come to me over the transom. All of my deals have been referred to me by a known and trusted third party who spoke highly of the company and the individuals involved with that company.

There is a process to raising money, which is almost universal for all early-stage investors. It begins with an executive summary or business plan. More often than not, an executive summary will suffice. This is a three to four page summary that outlines the problem the company is trying to solve, the founders, the management team, the technology, the market, the competition, and the financials. A company which is referred will always receive a closer look. If the firm is interested, the next step will be to pitch the group. This is typically a one-hour meeting with, at a maximum, thirty PowerPoint slides. The goal is to gain a high level understanding of the business, technology, and people. Expect a lot of questions. If that meeting goes well, the next step is due diligence. This is a deep dive into the business. If it is a healthcare company, this involves phoning clinicians, conducting management references, studying the intellectual property, and vetting the financials. Expect multiple visits to the company. The goal is to meet with the rest of the team and really try to get an understanding of what the company is all about.

If a company successfully makes it through the due diligence process, the next step would be to submit a term sheet. This is an indication the venture firm wants to invest and under what terms. A lengthy and sometimes heated negotiation will then occur. If the term sheet is accepted by both parties, it leads to the lawyers and the creation of the financing documents. After multiple iterations and more negotiating, the transaction hopefully closes. If this sounds like a long and laborious process, it is. Six to nine months is not unusual. Furthermore, the odds of getting to the finish line are low. Within healthcare alone, my firm will see over one thousand business plans a year. We will invest in five.

By reviewing over a thousand business plans per year, we as investors have a tremendous advantage. We are able to compare and contrast one company to the next. This provides a great perspective on what is going on in the marketplace. We track and monitor which companies are getting funded and which companies are not. It gives us a real sense for the type of deals that are getting done and which kind of new companies are getting started. Our active networking only strengthens this perspective. We go to conferences. We interact with the leading teaching hospitals. We talk to the technology transfer departments within the leading academic institutions. We have a group of technical and clinical advisors who help us understand what trends are emerging, what technologies are being developed, and what areas are hot. We draw heavily upon our networks to stay current and get ahead of the curve. It is our job to know what is going on out there and bring that perspective back to our companies, existing and new.

Growth Potential

A company's growth potential in healthcare is not always measured by the company's potential compounded annual growth rates. Rather, to determine growth potential, I focus on the company's ability to meet an unmet clinical need. If a problem is being solved and solved well, the growth will come. For example, a company developing a novel device to address cardiovascular disease is likely to target a huge problem. We know people still die from heart disease and thus we know unmet needs still remain. To identify such a company's growth potential, however, requires further digging. Clinically, I try to understand if the company's products will meet a clear need. If so, I try to determine the number of patients who would ultimately benefit from such a product. The next step is to determine the price per patient. The theoretical market potential can be determined by multiplying the two numbers together. Hopefully, it will be greater than $1 billion. Market penetration rates can then be assumed to project out revenues. My goal is to see a sales ramp in excess of $100 million within four to five years from launch. This kind of growth would provide a nice metric as to what I am seeking in potential sales growth. At the end of the day, it all circles back to unmet need and whether or not the company is solving a real problem.

Risk & Red Flags

The growth potential of a company is critically important, but it must always be balanced against the company's risk profile. Again, the higher the risk, the higher the desired reward. The level of risk an investor is willing to take is highly variable. It varies from firm to firm and partner to partner. I am personally comfortable taking technical and clinical risk. This risk can often be mitigated by hiring a strong management team early in the process. I have greater confidence a strong management team will successfully execute through the many challenges that will surface during a clinical trial. I am also a big believer in broadly syndicating deals with other venture firms. This helps to alleviate the financing risk. Broad syndication means investing side by side several venture firms. It can be difficult raising new money if a financing is required before a series of key milestones have been achieved. If these milestones are not achieved, an alternative strategy is to raise additional money from the existing investors. This interim financing, or inside round, can be used to fund the company until the appropriate milestones have been met. This approach, however, should not be considered a blank check. Even for an insider, real progress is required to a fund a company round to round.

As noted earlier, I am willing to take technical and clinical risk, however, I am less willing to take business model risk. At some point, these risks start to compound upon one another to a level where an investment becomes a non-starter. One, two, or even three major hurdles is expected, four, five, or six becomes daunting. A huge upside becomes a necessity given the low probability of success.

It is hard to build a company. Risks are inevitable. The goal, however, is to manage these risks. It does not mean shortchanging an opportunity.

From the outset, my goal is to always invest in a company with the belief that it will be a stand-alone entity with the potential to pursue an initial public offering. I look at investments as stand-alone opportunities with the desire to build a company, not a product. The pursuit of this strategy leads to the next truism: companies are acquired, they are not sold. As a company progresses, they often gain sufficient traction to attract the attention of several major acquirers. When an acquisition opportunity surfaces, a lengthy discussion ensues. Does the company sell early or go it alone? A number of factors come into play in making such a decision, however, price is always number one. After price, others question surface. Does the company have sufficient capital to make it over the finish line? Does the management team have the horsepower to keep going? Is the opportunity big enough to take the product to market ourselves? Can the company compete with the big boys? Again, the decision often comes down to a trade-off between risk and reward.

There are certainly a number of red flags I look for when I evaluate deals. If I ask the question, "Who is the competition," and the answer is, "There is none," that is a red flag. There always is competition. If a plan is not realistic, if the answers to questions are not thoughtful, if a team is overly optimistic, those are red flags. It tells me the team is either inexperienced or naive. Both are bad. There are also red flags in the way entrepreneurs respond to questions. If the individuals get irritated or the interaction turns hostile, I usually assume life is going to be tough when we work together. That is not the kind of interaction I want to see. Style is as important as substance. Negatives on either end can tank a deal. The last set of red flags has to do with the structure of the company itself. For example, did the first round of funding come from institutional investors or from a group of fifty angel investors? If it was the latter, that is a red flag. Companies that are burdened with too many angel investors often become challenging to work with down the road. There are too many individuals with too many expectations and not enough experience. Always a bad combination. It is hard enough to build a successful company. There is no reason to make it harder than it has to be. Clean deals are not only better, they are essential.

Questions for Entrepreneurs and Venture Capitalists

The number one question to ask an entrepreneur is "What problem are you trying to solve?" If it is a healthcare deal, what clinical need are you trying to meet? If it is a software deal, what problem are you trying to solve in the enterprise? Why does the company need to exist? From there, the questions will delve deeper into the business. Who is the competition? Why isn't the problem solved yet? Why isn't somebody else trying to solve the same problem? As we dig deeper yet, the next level of questioning begins. Why is your company better at solving that problem than anyone else? What is your unfair competitive advantage? Is it the technology, the management team, or some combination of both?

All of these questions are at a high level, but the answers help to characterize a particular business. Experience, and the fact that we are looking at thousands of plans, helps us assess if the plans are realistic or too optimistic. More often than not, capital projections are too low and the projected timelines are too short. Conservatism, with a healthy dose of optimism, provides the right blend of not too hard, not too soft.

Just as venture capitalists conduct due diligence on the entrepreneurs, the entrepreneurs should conduct due diligence on the venture capitalist. These are long-term relationships which can stretch out over five to seven years. The entrepreneur and the venture capitalist need to be able to work together. I personally encourage the entrepreneurs that I am interested in backing to call the other CEOs that I have backed and find out about myself. How do I operate on a board? What is it like to work with me? What is my style? Entrepreneurs should feel very comfortable doing their homework. At a minimum, entrepreneurs should ask for a list of the portfolio companies of a particular firm and determine whether or not we as a firm, and I as a partner, have the relevant experience. Another pertinent question regards the reserves of a fund. In particular, how much is my firm budgeting for subsequent rounds? More specifically, if my firm invests $5 million in the first round, does my fund have money in reserves for subsequent rounds. This can often be determined by knowing where the company sits within the fund's cycle. Is it the first investment or the last? Investments on the tail end of a fund can sometimes get shortchanged as companies which were funded earlier require more dollars than expected and cash at the fund level gets tight.

Success Defined

Successful companies are sustainable companies. These organizations have created a product that meets a clear need in the market. They continue to innovate and thereby continue to create value. Often, during a bubble, numerous companies will be formed and taken public. However, these companies are often gone a year later. Their success was based on a gold rush mentality, not on creating sustainable value. I believe success is defined by those companies who continue to grow, who continue to add new products, and ultimately who win in the marketplace. At a more granular level, successful companies are those who have established plans and willingly tossed those plans aside when the market demanded change. It has been said that 98 percent of all successful companies have had to change their business plan at some point in their life. Once again it is the management team who can make such changes. Good management teams are constantly evaluating the environment and adapting along the way. It is this ability to be nimble which allows for the ultimate creation of a successful company.

Building a successful enterprise is not a sprint, it is a marathon. There are stages which a company must cycle through. Develop a product, test the product, conduct clinicals, gain FDA approval, market the product, reach profitability. It is very difficult if not impossible to skip one of these stages. There are no shortcuts. In the late 1990s, the venture community was chasing the hot deals, the hot sectors. Nobody paid attention to prices. Valuations skyrocketed as investors paid up. The hope was you could invest in a company, build momentum, take the company public, and exit quickly. Of course hindsight is always 20/20. The venture community did not realize the crazy dynamics of the market until it was over. It was a new economy. Since then, the entrepreneurial community has gone back to basics. Companies are once again striving to build real value and investors are looking for real value. Prices are back in line. In fact, entrepreneurs may argue they are too low. Investors and management teams are trying to build companies on as little capital as possible. Capital was essentially free two years ago. It is very expensive today. Returns suffer if the capital requirements are too high. There are multiple measures of a successful company. Market share is one, return on investment is another. The most successful enterprises have achieved both.

Golden Rules and Essential Advice

As I have grown and learned the venture business, a number of folks have provided me with outstanding advice. Invest in good management teams. Invest with good people. Don't go it alone. Don't chase research projects. Look for large markets with clear unmet needs. Pursue clear business models. Preserve capital. Don't get greedy on the exit. Two stories, however, stand out as particularly relevant.

Before getting into the venture business and taking a role in a startup, I worked as a management consultant. As a consultant, I was often charged with helping companies develop their business plans and strategies. When I first entered the venture business, I had a tendency to want to rewrite the business plans I was reviewing. At times I would see an interesting product, but not agree with the direction of the company. I would come up with my own strategy and become quite enamored with the opportunity. One of my partners offered me some wise counsel. If success was predicated on my rewriting the plan, then the company was doomed to failure. It was doomed to failure because it was not my role. It was also doomed to failure because it was indicative of a management team who had not done their homework. Who had not fully thought through all of the issues. As a venture investor, I can only evaluate a team's thinking and influence that thinking once I have made an investment. I cannot reshape the plan. I am not close enough to the business. I am not living it day in and day out. I am micromanaging and that is the kiss of death for all involved.

This also leads to the next piece of great advice I received. Do good deals with good people. It sounds like basic advice, but it is the people dynamics of this business that can often kill a company. It is not only the interaction within a management team, but also the interaction between the entrepreneurs and the investors, the interaction between different board members and the interaction between different investors. It is important to work with people that are comfortable with one another and that have similar styles. At the same time, these individuals should be able to challenge and play off of one another. Again, my partner provided some wise advice. Find the best deals you can and work with the people you want to work with. The most exciting part of this business is the people. Not only my partners, but the entrepreneurs and the other investors. It is an extraordinarily talented group of people who know nothing but optimism. The business is always changing. Entrepreneurs are always inventing, always looking for new opportunities. It is an exciting group of folks to be around.

Michael Carusi, General Partner, joined Advanced Technology Ventures in 1998. He provides strategic leadership and insight for emerging companies in the life sciences and medical device sectors. Founded in 1979, Advanced Technology Ventures (ATV) is a leading venture capital firm whose management experience, technology expertise, global network of industry contacts and collaborative style has helped more than 120 companies navigate from inception to IPO and beyond. With approximately $1.5 billion of committed capital, its portfolio includes investments in the areas of communications, Internet infrastructure, software and services, and healthcare. ATV's investment philosophy centers on collaborative, active participation with the management teams of its portfolio companies. ATV's healthcare portfolio benefits from Mike's significant domain expertise and strong industry relationships, a result of his ten years of experience in operations and management consulting.

Mike currently serves on the Boards of ATV portfolio companies Optobionics, Percardia, deNovis, MicroVention and Emphasys Medical.

Prior to joining ATV, Mike served as the Director of Business Development for Inhale Therapeutic Systems, a venture-backed pulmonary drug delivery company that went public in 1994. Mike was also a Principal at The Wilkerson Group, a strategic ATV partner and leading management consulting firm focused exclusively on health care.

Mike earned an MBA from the Amos Tuck School of Business Administration at Dartmouth College and a BS in Mechanical Engineering from Lehigh University.

The 2 Best Selling Venture Capital Titles of the Year

Term Sheets & Valuations – A Line by Line Look at Venture Capital Term Sheets and Valuations

ISBN 1-58762-068-5, By Alex Wilmerding, $14.95

Term Sheets & Valuations is the first ever in-depth look at the nuts and buts of terms sheets and valuations. The book, written by leading venture capitalist Alexander Wilmerding of Boston Capital Ventures, covers topics such What is a Term Sheet, How to Examine a Term Sheet, A Section-by-Section View of a Term Sheet, Valuations, What Every Entrepreneur & Executive Needs to Know About Term Sheets, Valuation Parameters, and East Coast Versus West Coast Rules. In addition, the book includes an actual term sheet from a leading law firm with line by line descriptions of each clause, what can/should be negotiated, and the important points to pay attention to. A must have book for any executive, entrepreneur, or financial professional.

Praise for Term Sheets & Valuations: "This primer should be required reading for every entrepreneur. It is short, authoritative and worth its weight in gold." - Murray Low, Executive Director, Columbia Business School, Eugene M. Lang Center for Entrepreneurship

"An invaluable resource for executives and financial professionals." - Graham D.S. Anderson, General Partner, EuclidSR Partners

Deal Terms - The Finer Points of Venture Capital Deal Structures, Valuations, Term Sheets, Stock Options and Getting Deals Done

ISBN 1-58762-208-4, By Alex Wilmerding, $49.95

Deal Terms is the first ever in-depth look at valuations, preferred stock, stock options and other variables that affect deal structure, written by Alex Wilmerding (a venture capitalist at Boston Capital Ventures and best selling author of Term Sheets & Valuations). Written from a venture capital perspective, however applicable for all types of financings, Deal Terms includes actual term sheets, valuation methodology and analysis, assessment of stock option programs and their impact on valuations and capital structures and other real world documents used by leading venture capitalists and lawyers analyzed from multiple perspectives. A must have book for any executive, entrepreneur, or financial professional, this timeless classic is an unprecedented resource that will help you avoid costly mistakes, understand various structures and terms, and understand wording and language from other deal sheets to help you get deals done.

Praise for Deal Terms: "Deal terms are a huge issue for most entrepreneurs; this is a really important resource." Andrew McKee, General Partner, Webster Capital

"An indispensable reference for entrepreneurs and finance professionals...", Clifford Schorer, Entrepreneur in Residence, Columbia Business School

To Order or For Customized Suggestions From an Aspatore Business Editor, Please Call 1-866-Aspatore (277-2867) Or Visit www.Aspatore.com

VC FORUM

THE QUARTERLY JOURNAL WHERE LEADERS INTERACT

Trying to stay a step ahead of the key issues every venture capital professional needs to be aware of? Interested in interacting with a community of senior venture capitalists, entrepreneurs and executives from the world's top firms? For only $195 a year, subscribe today to VC Forum, the quarterly journal for the senior most intelligence with respect to the venture capital business.

Sample VC Forum and Aspatore Published Authors Include:

Michael Moritz, Partner, Sequoia Capital
Heidi Roizen, Partner, Softbank
David J. Cowan, GP, Bessemer Venture Partners
Anthony Sun, Co-CEO & Managing General Partner, Venrock
Lawrence E. Mock, Jr., President & CEO, Mellon Ventures, Inc.
Terry McGuire, Co-Founder & Managing General Partner, Polaris
Graham Anderson, General Partner, EuclidSR Partners
Oliver D. Curme, General Partner, Battery Ventures
Jonathan Goldstein, Partner, TA Associates
Suzanne King, Partner, New Enterprise Associates
Mathias Schilling, Partner, Bertelsmann Ventures
Praveen Gupta, Partner, CDIB Ventures
Michael Carusi, GP, Advanced Technology Ventures
Mark Macenka, Testa Hurwitz & Thiebeault, Business Chair
Patrick Ennis, Arch Venture Partners, Partner
Gerard DiFiore, Reed Smith, Corporate Group Head
Sam Colella, Versant Ventures, Managing Director
Robert Chefitz, Apax Partners, General Partner
Daniel H. Bayly, Merrill Lynch, Chairman of Investment Banking
Eduardo Mestre, Salomon Smith Barney, Vice Chairman, Investment Banking

VC Forum is a quarterly journal that enables professionals connected to venture capital to cover all their knowledge bases and participate as a member of a community of leading executives. VC Forum is an interactive journal, the content of which is provided exclusively by its readership, and upon subscribing, new members become eligible to submit articles for possible publication in the journal. While other venture related resources focus on current events, specific industries, or funded deals, VC Forum helps professionals stay one step ahead of major venture related trends that are occurring 3 to 6 months from now.

With only 24 hours in a day, venture related professionals are expected to have a sound understanding of every aspect of the business, be aware of all major economic trends, and keep up with constant changes in the corporate world as a whole – a task that would be impossible without the appropriate resources. Each quarterly issue features articles on the core areas of which every venture related professional must be aware, in order to stay one step ahead - including trends in valuations, management teams, governance, exit strategies, M&A, tax and legal strategies, and more. Over the course of the year, VC Forum features the thinking of executives from over half the top 250 leading venture capital firms, investors in venture capital funds, investment bankers, entrepreneurs from VC funded companies, legal and accounting venture capital related specialists around the world.

To Order or For Customized Suggestions From an Aspatore Business Editor, Please Call 1-866-Aspatore (277-2867) Or Visit www.Aspatore.com

Inside the Minds:
The Ways of the VC

Acknowledgements & Dedications

David Cowan – The editors of this book asked me to address a series of questions that entrepreneurs might have about venture investors. The thoughts that I share in my chapter represent some of the many things I have learned over the years from my partner and mentor, Dr. Felda Hardymon at Harvard Business School.

Praveen Gupta – I dedicate my chapter to my wife Reeta and my son Ankur for their support in achieving my goals, and to my parents – J. P. and Kanti Vaish for being my mentors.